Publish. Promote. Profit.
Rob Kosberg

ISBN: 978-1-946978-86-8

Dedication

To Connie, Niko, Jake and Cole. You are my inspiration and the reason I do what I do.

To my amazing team at BSP, what would I do without you? That's a rhetorical question, I do not want to find out. Thank you for your tireless service to our clients.

Publish. Promote. Profit.™

Rob Kosberg

BEST SELLER
PUBLISHING

A GIFT FOR YOU!

Discover how our **Publish. Promote. Profit.**™ program has helped over 500 business owners, speakers, coaches and consultants become Best-Selling Authors.

Access a **Bonus Video Training** on the 3 steps necessary to publish, promote and then profit from your best selling book.

But wait there's more...

* Also get this FREE BONUS: Get Booked on TV, Radio and Media Training. ($997 Value) Includes video training, TV segment proposal template, Example booking script, Top 100 Radio and

TV show contact list.
All yours FREE with this book.

DON'T WAIT

**Watch this FREE VIDEO TRAINING now,
and learn how YOU can Become the Hunted!**
http://publishpromoteprofit.com/free

Contents

Praise for Rob and Best Seller Publishing

I first met Rob and Best Seller Publishing 3 years ago when I was looking for a publisher and marketing expert for my book anthology series, *"Put a Shark in your Tank"*. Rob became a friend, trusted adviser and later a partner with me on our new book series. The strategies and tactics Rob teaches in this book are truly cutting edge and what's working right now with him and his clients, including me. Rob outlines the strategies necessary to not just have great content but to get your content into the hands of your ideal client and build yourself a platform and legacy with it. In this book Rob shows you how to go from hunting for clients to being *The Hunted*.

I am thrilled to see this content get into the hands of those with a message that the world needs to hear. As I was once told I now tell you. It's time to leave the shadows and make an impact with your message. Here's to building your legacy.

- KEVIN HARRINGTON
Inventor of the Infomercial and original Shark on ABC's Shark Tank,
Best Selling Author of Put A Shark In Your Tank

Writing a book is a process that for some of us invokes every emotion imaginable, from insecurity to elation, the range of feelings are vast. No one can confidently tackle such a process of self-publishing alone and emerge with an Amazon #1 Best Seller in multiple categories... Unless you work with Best Seller Publishing.

As one of their past clients, I started only with my unfinished manuscript. It had been 2 years in the making. I shopped around to traditional publishers and found them more interested in having me buy my own books than selling them for me. Further, I was a first time author with few "connections" in the publishing world. And, I didn't want to give up any of the rights to my own work, which is common with traditional publishers.

Then one day I was introduced to Rob Kosberg who's own story of starting a business based on one self-published book, and the lessons learned from that process, convinced me that I needed his company's help.

From manuscript submission to #1 Amazon author, the entire process took about 45 days. They did everything; they designed the cover, the interior layout, the marketing, the launch, the P/R and the follow through. For what I paid to have Best Seller Publishing get my book to #1 Status, it was a screaming bargain. My book: The Invisible Organization has become my identity in the business world and raises my credibility immensely, as any business book will do for the author.

If you are investigating self-publishing then check them out, they have an unparalleled track record of success.

- MITCH RUSSO
Former CEO of Tony Robbins co., Business Breakthroughs,
*Best Selling Author of **The Invisible Organization***

Rob has a system that works, he takes a personal interest in his authors and to me it is a one stop shop that was a savings of time, energy and money and also helped move this project forward in a very efficient way. My thanks go out to Rob and BSP because they did help make my book a BEST SELLER.

- DELANO LEWIS
Former U.S. Ambassador to South Africa,
*Best Selling Author of **It All Begins With Self***

I just wanted to give a thanks to Rob for the work done in helping me become a best selling author. I now have 2 books that have gone to #1 in Amazon! This positions me as the expert in my field and gives me the credibility that I need to grow my coaching and continue me forward in my career. So thank you for all the hard work done to catapult me to the next level.

- JIM HANSEN
Former CEO of Franchising, Subway International,
*Best Selling Author of **Secrets of Choosing A Franchise***

This company pretty much launched my speaking and publishing career. I had been struggling for many years as a Speaker and Author. No one had heard of me. I lacked confidence because I was living in the shadows of my business. I was a published author with practically zero sales in books. Then Best Seller Publishing came along and took my second book to #1 best seller on Amazon. That's when everything took off in my business. Not only did my confidence grow, I increased my speaking engagements and my book sales increased as a result.

Best Seller publishing does not make promises it does not keep. You get exactly what is stated in the agreement. This is a company with integrity. I owe a lot of my business success to them, and I'm glad that I made the initial business investment with them.

More GREAT NEWS. My book not only made #1 best seller, it also made #1 in Hot New Releases and #1 in Top Rated Books in Amazon. Thank you, Rob! There is that one person in your life that changes the course and trajectory of your existence. You are that one person for me.

- Dr. NICOLINE AMBE
*Harvard Lecturer, Best Selling Author of **Above & Beyond***

"I wanted to take my business to a whole new level but just didn't know how to get there then I found Rob Kosberg and the best selling author program. They did all the marketing for me and my book (Conquer your closing) and all I had to do was sit there and watch my book climb in ranking (all the way to #1). It's so exciting – I can tell you there was a lot of screaming going on around here! Within 24 hours of my book going to #1 I received an invitation to be a paid speaker at a national real estate convention – and that's exactly where I want to be. So if you want to take your business to a whole new level then I believe a best selling book is the answer.

- KAREN SIMPSON-HANKINS
Best Selling Author of
Conquer Your Closing

What an exciting week as Best Seller Publishing took me to becoming Amazon Bestseller in 7 countries with over 3,000 downloads. I couldn't have done it without them. They are the best! If you are looking for a publishing team who will walk you through each step, deliver with authenticity and bring you results beyond your wildest dreams, give Bestseller Publishing a call. I highly recommend them.

- LINDA OLSON
Best Selling Author of
Your Story Matters!

Working with BSP is hands down one of the best decisions I have made! They are absolutely incredible to work with!

- ERICA ORMSBY
TEDx Speaker, Best Selling Author of
I Am Happy. Healthy. Free.

I almost can't believe how easy this has been! I met Rob at the end of 2016, the idea of a book, let alone an International Best Seller book seemed so far from possible that I'd barely given it a thought. 6 months later, AND IT'S A REALITY! Rob's team make the process effortless - they are such a well oiled machine that, from the authors point of view, it really is just write and then trust that the process will work! Everything they promised has come to fruition, and I have no doubt that the remaining publicity part of my journey with Best Seller Publishing will be just as exciting and easy as the first publishing phase!

- BREE STEDMAN
TEDx Speaker, Best Selling Author of
Own Your BS

From first contact to the completion of my book, the entire team has been amazing to work with. They were supportive, guiding, and responsive during the entire process. I could not have asked for better representation and guidance through this process. I am a first time author and would highly recommend this team for anyone who has a desire to write and successfully publish their book.

- DR. DARLA LOGAN
Best Selling Author of
Regenerative Medicine

Oh, my gosh! These people are absolutely amazing! They are extremely professional, courteous, caring and hard-working! I am so glad that I used Best Seller Publishing to publish my first book. The results have been astonishing. Thank you to the BSP Team. You are the best!

- SCOTT KIMBRO
Best Selling Author of
SubmUrgency

The Best Seller Publishing team was a pleasure to work with. Their patience and professionalism made the intimidating task of publishing enjoyable.

I appreciate their attention to detail and their accesibilty. It has taken me YEARS to build up the courage and discipline to pen my initial thoughts, but in a short time this team helped to birth this book and the experience has encouraged and inspired me to write many more.

Thank you Best Seller Publishing. You guys rock!

- TONY E. SANDERS JR.
Best Selling Author of
Daddy Talks

These guys are so great! They deliver exactly what they promise and they make the whole process so easy! Strongly recommend working with them- especially for first time authors!

- CANDICE SETI
Best Selling Author of
Shatter The Yoyo

Becoming an International Best Selling Author was never in my reachable thoughts because I could not imagine where or how to begin! Yet, I always had the yearning to write a book because I believe that life-stories are the sage of society. With the help of Best Seller Publishing and their fantastic staff; I now have a dream come true that I never dreamt possible! Rob, Randy, Sydney, Ilana, Rebecca, Steve, Melissa....naming gets me in trouble! The ENTIRE team! If you are looking for a company to work with you in this space - look no further! Trust the process, trust the team, and trust the story that needs birthing inside of you to Best Seller Publishing! Before you know it, you'll be like me...a new international best selling author... WOW! Thanks BSP. I look forward to remaining engaged as we move into the profit phase of "publish, promote, profit!"

- DR. BRENDA J. BOWERS
Best Selling Author of
World Changers & Difference Makers

I give Best Seller Publishing 5 ✳ stars!! They are a great company that follows through on what they say they are going to accomplish. They treat us like family and are very helpful. They have a lot of information to learn how to further and improve yourself and book sales. They are the real deal that gets your book to best seller status.

- JILL DAVIS
Best Selling Author of
Alaska Man

Writing your first book is an idea that needs a lot of help to come to fruition. Working with Best Sellers Publishing was the right move and i'm glad I started from day one with Rob and his team. Helped me get the ideas out of my head and into print. Then guided me right into best seller status. Couldn't recommend them more.

- RODNEY KOOP
Best Selling Author of
Why Won't they Pay Me What I'm Worth?

I am so glad I chose BSP as my Team to Publish, Promote, and Profit my 20+ years' experience in working with Baby Boomers and Beyond! I love the systematic way they guide you through the process. I had already written copy compiling information I have used in seminars I teach, so their method of assembling the material into a best-selling book was incredible! I've been introduced to a group of professionals who guided me seamlessly through the process of transforming my seminars into a best-selling book! I couldn't be happier! Thanks to Head Guru Rob Kosberg, Sydney, Steve, Rebecca and everyone else! I'm looking forward to writing another book!

- DEBBIE MILLER
Best Selling Author of **Move Or Improve?**

Rob is an excellent teacher and knows his craft extremely well. I highly recommend attending his Million Dollar Author Summit. The content is on point for any aspiring author. He also knows when to bring in speakers and ties their message into this teachings better then any conference I have attended. Thank you for the opportunity!

- MARK VILLAREAL
Best Selling Author of **Leadership Lessons From Mom**

I have been working with Best Seller Publishing since the fall of 2015 to publish my book, Bulletproof Your Marriage. Their team is amazing and through their efforts, Bulletproof Your Marriage became an international best seller in 3 categories. Additionally, it has won international accolades as a finalist in the Parenting and Family category of Bookvana International Book Awards.

We are just entering the Publicity phase of their program and I am excited about the results we will see.

If you have a book that you want to write, or have written, you owe it to yourself to reach out to Best Seller Publishing to assist you in writing and launching your book. You will be glad you did. I know that I am thrilled with the results my book has achieved thus far.

- REGINA PARTAIN
Best Selling Author of **Bulletproof Your Marriage**

"Best Seller Publishing" made my "Little Book about Big Body Transformation" a best seller. It's a team of dedicated professionals. If you want to write a book and make it a best seller don't look any further. It was my passion to write a book, and Rob Kosberg as a true leader made me think outside the box, showing a bigger perspective of business opportunities a bestselling book could provide me. I would highly recommend this business to my friends and family. Thank you guys! Keep it up!

\- OLGA AHRENS
Best Selling Author of **Little Book About Big Body Transformation**

Rob and his team are first class when it comes to service and results. My book, Mind Over Market, became a Number One Best Seller is 2 categories on amazon. Their publicity team also had me on several of the top real estate podcasts in the country, and published in a top real estate publication. If you're going to write a book, don't be some one who puts it off...hire these guys and watch your success soar!

\- TAMARA DORRIS
Best Selling Author of **Mind Over Market**

Wonderful experience! Rob and the entire BSP team (Randy, Sydney, Steve, Rebecca, Austin, Ilana) is excellent to work with and they deliver with what they promise. Any time I had a question, someone was there to answer quickly. BSP is results driven and they truly care about the people they work with. This is something that sets them apart from others in the industry. I would happily recommend BSP to any serious service based professional who aspires to write a best selling book. With expert marketing from BSP our book became an International #1 Best Seller in multiple categories on the very first day!

\- RICHARD PERRY
Best Selling Author of **It's Not Just About the Money**

I just want to thank Rob Kosberg and his fantastic staff at Best Seller Publishing. They have accomplished in weeks what I probably could never have accomplished in years by helping me to be come an International Best Seller for my book The Biggest Short Guy. Their knowledge, guidance, and fantastic attitude has made the decision of working with them one of the best decision I've ever made on both a personal and business level. And the amazing part is, we are early in the process. Thanks so much Best Seller Publishing your a best performer.

- JIM BERAN
Best Selling Author of **The Biggest Short Guy**

As a retired U.S. Special Agent, I had wanted to write a book based on my experience and expertise to help others. Rob Kosberg and his dynamic team at "Best Seller Publishing" made the process simple and provided me with an outstanding book that became a # 1 Best Seller. His team also helped me to be interviewed on ABC, CBS, NBC, and Fox News. If you're looking to write a book to help promote yourself and your business, then I highly recommend you contact "Best Seller Publishing". Rob and his team are the real deal!

- KEVIN CRANE
Best Selling Author of **Access Granted**

I love the creative process of a book, but the little details around content and then the marketing always caused me to stop. But this year I found Best Seller Publishing who helped me with the all the details so I could do what I do best, and just today in hit International Best Seller! Can't say enough good things!

- MIA MORAN
Best Selling Author of **Plan Simple Meals**

I have worked with Best Seller Publishing on two different books, and each has achieved best seller status.

The second one, I also chose the path to do TV and podcast promotions, and it has opened a ton of doors for me.

The staff is superb, and they really care about what they do. I had a great experience and have referred several clients to Rob and his team.

- HALEY GRAY
*Best Selling Author of **Leadership Girl***

Although I can't recall exactly how we connected initially, I was very clear on what I wanted: A #1 Bestseller book so that I could use that as an entree into other ventures. It provides instant credibility, if one knows how to use it right. I wrote a short book about my life as an alcoholic, drug addict, loser father (then), horrible husband (then), financial failure (then), and thoroughly enjoyed the experience. I know I'm not using it to it's potential, and BSP has stayed in touch with me, helped me move forward in various areas (sans fee), and I value the relationship as one of the first and best of my new life. Life Rocks!

- BRIAN WACIK
*Best Selling Author of **Life Rocks!***

Best Seller Publishing did a FANTASTIC job taking what I had as plans for my book and turning it into a International Best Seller! They helped me every step of the way and I wouldn't be where I am at today without them. I cannot Thank them enough for all they have done for me. Plus they are getting me on TV and podcasts. Rock on and Keep up the Great Work!

- JO HAUSMAN
*Best Selling Author of **Go For It!***

Rob and his team went above and beyond. Never have a met such a dedicated team that is truly in your corner. They've delivered on every promise made and I would highly recommend them to anyone who wants to write, publish and take their book to the next level!

- COREY GLADWELL
Best Selling Author of
The Human Experience

Working with Best Seller Publishing was great! I had a fantastic editor in Sunniva, a great designer in Steve, and rockstars like Sydney, Rebecca, Randy and Michelle all helping my book to be the best it could be AND helping me launch and make it a #1 Best-Seller in multiple categories in multiple countries! It was awesome having an entire team behind me to help my dreams of becoming a published author come true! Thanks gals and guys!

- JASON GOLDBERG
TEDx Speaker, Best Selling Author of
Prison Break

Rob and his team were awesome. Not only was my book an international best seller after they were done, but they got me on TV, radio, podcasts, and other promotional spots to monetize what I had done with the book. Thanks, Best Seller Publishing team!

- FRANK BRIA
*Best Selling Author of **Scale***

I have worked with Best Seller Publishing over the past year. They helped me take an idea for a book (The Depression Miracle) and turn it into an International Best Seller within a few months. They are the real deal and have over delivered on everything they promised me from day one. I can't say enough good things about Rob Kosberg and his team!

- GREG THREDGOLD
Best Selling Author of **The Depression Miracle**

Rob & his team @ Best Seller Publishing are everything you need to help you navigate common obstacles to successfully publishing and promoting your book . In just 6 short months, we have experienced a 4x increase in revenue, and secured a national speaking engagement. We would enthusiastically recommend BSP for publishing your book.

- JOEL LANDI
Best Selling Author of **Rewired**

Preface

A few years ago, I was out to dinner with one of my friends and we were talking about our businesses. And while we were there, we were watching our kids playing out on the playground, and we were sharing ideas, and at the end he said,

> *"You know what the difference is between you and guys like Tony Robbins and Brendon Burchard?"*
>
> *"No, what?" I said, genuinely curious.*
>
> *"I personally feel like your content is better. The things you share are more applicable. But the difference between them and you? The reason why they are bigger than you? They have a book and you don't."*

At first I was upset, but then as I thought about it more, I realized…he was right. Even though I published a tremendous amount of content and courses, I never took the time and effort to sit down and write a book.

That night, I decided to start. I had been thinking about writing a book for almost a decade, but that night it began.

I spent the next few months writing the book, getting it published, and launching it. After writing that book, I swore I would never write another one again, but now that it was done, I was excited to launch it and get it into the hands of my customers.

We did the book launch and sold tens of thousands of copies. But what happened next was totally unexpected and amazing.

Not only did publishing a book help me strengthen relationships with existing customers, it got me into new markets that were previously unavailable to me.

This book broke down walls, built up new relationships, and grew my business in ways nothing else had been able to.

In fact, it worked so well, that within a year of publishing the first book (and swearing I would never write another), I started writing my second book, Expert Secrets.

Then, we launched that book and my brand expanded even more, my business continued to grow exponentially, as well as my ability to serve my customers at the highest level possible.

Right now, at the time of writing of this forward, I'm working on the outline of my next book. In fact, this morning, I was at a used bookstore with some of my friends, and I told them, "You all should be writing a book. Even if you're not writing one yet, when anyone asks you, say you're writing a book."

There is something about moving towards that direction. You'll get more enjoyment out of learning, get more clarity with your message, and feel more fulfilled as you help the lives of those around you.

Rob is helping authors and people who want to become authors for the last decade. I've had a chance to know him about half that time. I've seen him help hundreds and hundreds of people to turn their expertise and passions into books.

The book is one of the most powerful business tools out there. On top of that, I personally believe it's also one of the best personal development tools for you as well. You will grow as a human being and you will be able to serve and impact more people around you with your message.

I'm excited for you to start this journey to get your book written.

Thanks
- RUSSELL BRUNSON
Founder, Clickfunnels

Foreword

This book couldn't be more timely. With the growth of Amazon and self-publishing It has never been easier to publish a book. What many people don't realize though is that means it's never been easier to fail at it as well. Over 1,000,000 books will be published this year alone and as I learned reading through Rob's book the vast majority of them will languish in obscurity, regardless of the quality of the content. It doesn't need to be that way.

I know firsthand the power of a best-selling book. My first 25 years in business consisted of me being behind the camera as the pioneer and inventor of the informercial. I had the great fortune to help bring to the world amazing products like the Ginsu knife (remember that!) and Tony Little Fitness as well as work with amazing entrepreneurs like George Foreman and Jack Lalane. Over $5 Billion in sales and not a single person knew my name.

That began to change after a conversation with a friend and mentor, Richard Branson. As the founder and CEO of Virgin, Richard is well known and sought after as the face of his company. His advice was that I leave the shadows and rather than building others brands I should become a brand myself. Hard to disagree with a billionaire, so I decided to write my first book, *"Act Now! : How I Turn Ideas Into Million-Dollar Products"*.

That book ended up on the desk of Mark Burnett, television producer of the hit show, *Survivor*. Though I didn't know Mark he reached out to me personally because he had an idea for a new entrepreneurial reality show called, *Shark Tank*. Though initially apprehensive (because I saw what they did to those people on the island) I flew out to Los Angeles to meet with him and became the first "Shark" for what would become one of the hottest new reality show on TV. Since then I have gone from completely behind the scenes to being recognized worldwide and sought after as a top 3 business speaker by Forbes Magazine. And it all started with my first book.

I first met Rob and Best Seller Publishing 3 years ago when I was looking for a publisher and marketing expert for my book anthology series, *"Put a Shark in your Tank"*. Rob became a friend, trusted adviser and later a partner with me on our new book series. The strategies and tactics Rob teaches in this book are truly cutting edge and what's working right now with him and his clients, including me. Rob outlines the strategies necessary to not just have great content but to get your content into the hands of your ideal client and build yourself a platform and legacy with it. In this book Rob shows you how to go from hunting for clients to being *The Hunted*.

I am thrilled to see this content get into the hands of those with a message that the world needs to hear. As I was once told I now tell you. It's time to leave the shadows and make an impact with your message. Here's to building your legacy.

- KEVIN HARRINGTON
Inventor of the Infomercial and original
Shark on ABC's Shark Tank.

Introduction

"If Stupidity got us into this mess,
then why can't it get us out?"

—**Will Rogers**

I was in a mess!

"What would you do if you were in a situation like me?" I asked.

"Well, if I had to start over and rebuild a business in a brand-new industry, like you're having to do, I would write a book."

"Really? A book?" I questioned.

At that point I'd never really thought of writing a book but, why would I? I had been in real estate on and off since I was 18 years old. and the three real estate companies that I owned in 2006 closed over $100 million in transactions. I was also heavily invested in real estate and, hey, what could go wrong?

Right!? What could go wrong?

I still remember when I realized that the mortgage meltdown and the crash of my businesses were inevitable. It was September 2007 and our biggest lenders, American Home Mortgage and American Brokers Conduit, had closed the doors and stopped funding loans.

Overnight, 7,000 employees were laid off. They were our biggest lender-funding mortgages for our executive properties and investments in South Florida.

My business at that point was in free fall, not able to fund loans, not able to close deals, and watching real estate values plummet as much as 60 percent in affluent areas in South Florida.

There I was, in early 2008, closing the doors to my business and laying off dozens of employees of a business that just a year earlier had been one of the most successful in the area.

As I sit back and think about that time right now, I still feel some of the same emotions I experienced then, even though that was 10 years ago. The fear I had in my early 40s of having to start over and wondering exactly how I was going to do it.

Today, I am so thankful that I took that advice and wrote my first book, *Life After Debt: Practical Solutions to Get Out of Debt, Build Wealth, and Radically Transform Your Finances Forever!* That little book became the number-one nonfiction book on all of Amazon, outselling everyone from Tony Robbins to Dave Ramsey. More important (just being honest), it was responsible for millions of dollars in income. In the worst economy in my generation, it produced over a million dollars in revenue for a brand-new business *in the first year alone.*

Product Details
File Size: 920 KB
Print Length: 76 pages
Simultaneous Device Usage: Unlimited
Publisher: www.BestSellerPublishing.org (September 24, 2012)
Sold by: Amazon Digital Services, Inc.
Language: English
ASIN: B009G8ITBW
Text-to-Speech: Enabled
X-Ray: Enabled
Word Wise: Enabled
Lending: Enabled
Amazon Best Sellers Rank: #12 Paid in Kindle Store (See Top 100 Paid in Kindle Store)
#1 in Books > Business & Money > Personal Finance > **Budgeting & Money Management**
#1 in Kindle Store > Kindle eBooks > Business & Money > Personal Finance > Budgeting & Money Management > **Budgeting**
#1 in Kindle Store > Kindle eBooks > Business & Money > Personal Finance > Budgeting & Money Management > **Money Management**

LAD Sales Ranking

Since that time, I've had the opportunity to be featured in everything, from *Forbes*, *Entrepreneur*, to TV and radio, and in speaking engagements to audiences of over 5,000 people. Me!? Yep, little ole me.

Because of the success with my first book, people started coming to me to see if they could also see the incredible results from writing a book that I did. After all, maybe I just got lucky? Well, if that's the case then almost 500 other new authors have also "just gotten lucky!"

After a couple of years of helping authors, I decided I enjoyed it more than finance and sold my financial services company and started Best Seller Publishing (BSP). Again, another multimillion-dollar business was born, all on the back of writing a book.

I don't know what your reasons are for wanting to write a book. Perhaps you're looking to start over, exactly like I did. Perhaps you've been wanting to write a book for years and haven't been able to for one reason or another, or perhaps you want to take your business and your life, your authority, your credibility to the next level.

Well, I'm here to tell you that the absolute greatest thing you can do for your business and for your life, for you personally and for your family, is to write your book. As I sit here today, there's been nothing in my business life that has helped transform it more than writing my book.

In the pages of this book, you're going to learn exactly what BSP does for our clients, to make their dreams a reality.

We've worked hard to make sure that nothing is left out and that we give you all the information you need to write your transformational work, make it a bestseller, and for it to lead to incredible things for you, for your business and for future books that you write and sell.

Here's to your journey!

CHAPTER 1

Why a Book?
(My Big Break)

"Life isn't about finding yourself.
Life is about creating yourself."

—George Bernard Shaw

I think you'll be happy to know that I made every mistake imaginable with my book. From paying a ghostwriter a huge amount of money and getting absolute garbage (more about that later) to believing some of the book-marketing experts out there and paying for one-off services, like press releases or email drops, all with zero results.

In the midst of challenges (which you will absolutely face), you have two options to choose from. It's either time to decide what you really believe about a best selling book and double down on your commitment or, quite frankly, give up the project all together.

Gary Keller of Keller Williams Realty International has something to say about this. The first book he wrote was called *The Millionaire Real Estate Agent: It's Not about the Money . . . It's about Being the Best You Can Be!* He has gone on to write many other books since then. Recently I was reading one of his books, titled *The One Thing: The Surprisingly Simple Truth behind Extraordinary Results.*

On page 40 of his book, he relates how he came up with the idea to write a book. He says,

> *In 2001, I called a meeting of our key executive team. As fast as we were growing, we were still not acknowledged by the very top people in our industry. I challenged our group to brainstorm 100 ways to turn this situation around. It took us all day to come up with the list. The next morning, we narrowed the list down to ten ideas, and from there we chose just one big idea. The one that we decided on was that I would write a book on how to become an elite performer in our industry. It worked. Eight years later that one book had not only become a national bestseller, but also had morphed into a series of books with total sales of over a million copies. In an industry of about a million people, one thing changed our image forever.*

Today, Keller Williams is the largest real estate brokerage in the world, and Gary Keller is a billionaire. Did it work for him? Was there magic in a book for him?

> I believe there is magic in a book for almost anyone looking to grow a business and explode their income and impact.

I also believed there was magic for me in a book. I believe there is magic in a book for almost anyone looking to grow a business and explode their income and impact.

The magic isn't found just in the words that we put on the page and the expertise that we give our audience. The magic is found in how we're viewed because of the book. See the illustration about what I call the hierarchy of desire. I'm probably not the first to present this idea, and I certainly won't be the last. However, the concept of the hierarchy of desire is that as your celebrity increases in the eyes of your ideal client, so too does your attractiveness and how much you can charge.

The magic is in how your book propels you from generalist or even specialist to expert, and eventually thought leader and celebrity.

And, as we like to say at BSP, you go from hunting for clients to becoming the hunted. Let me explain my big break, if you will.

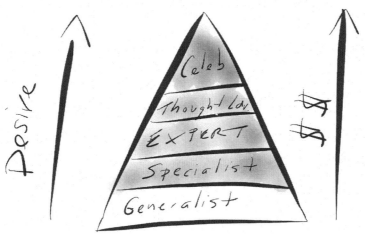

Hierarchy of Desire

After all the aforementioned mistakes and far too long in coming, quite frankly, I finally had my book done, but wondered, now what. I didn't exactly know what to do, other than knowing that I needed to get my book into people's hands.

Mind you, this is all before podcasting, Facebook, Twitter, or any social media, for that matter. (It is so much easier for us to communicate our message today).

So, what did I do? I began sending my books to local radio stations and suggesting that they have me on their radio shows as a financial authority. After all, I was a bestselling author on the topic, and I could discuss the financial trauma and difficulties that many of their listeners were going through at the time.

After sending my book, I would follow-up with a telephone call to the local radio station manager. I kept following up until finally landing my first interview on a local station.

The interview was a standard four to five minutes, with the interviewer asking me questions and me presenting options for people financially. The interview went well and at the end of that five-minute spot I offered anyone who was interested in learning more and getting help a free copy of my bestselling book. In fact, I would even pay the shipping, there was no charge whatsoever.

This was long before the idea of free-plus-shipping funnels that we see online now, which, by the way, we'll talk more about. I knew that if I could speak directly to people who had these challenges, then I could present solutions for them and perhaps they would become clients of mine.

The radio interview was done live, and the station also played the recording several other times during the day. The first night it aired, I was in my office by myself about 6:00 p.m. and the phone rang.

I answered the phone, and said, "This is Rob, how may I help you?"

The person on the other line simply said, "Is this Rob Kosberg?"

My first thought was, *Oh, man, I hope this isn't somebody I owe money to* (insert humor, kinda). Remember it was shortly after my real estate business collapse.

I said, "Yes, this is Rob, how can I help you?"

She said, "Wow, I can't believe I'm actually speaking to you. This is Rob Kosberg, the author and the person I heard on the radio, right?

And I said, "Why yes, yes, it is. ☺

At that moment I personally experienced the magic of a book. I had never met this person, yet she had heard me on the radio, heard about my book, and because of that saw me as an authority and perhaps even as a celebrity. We spoke for about 20 minutes, and she became a client that night. No hardcore sales techniques were needed. No special closes. She needed help, and I was the authority who could help her.

I thought, *Maybe I'm on to something here?*

I started doing more radio interviews. I started spending a little bit of money on paid radio ads, and after about eight months, I even had my own radio show. Within a year, I was doing four hours of live radio every single week, offering my book for free (and shipped for free) to get it into people's hands.

I learned that for every 16 books we gave away, at a cost of about $5 shipped, we brought on a new client that was worth over $6,000 to my company. We exchanged about $80 (plus the cost of the radio advertising) to make a $6,000 sale. How many times would you like to do that?

> Your book, your bestselling book, is your gateway to greater authority, celebrity, and client attraction.

We did over a million dollars in the first year (in a terrible economy) and then multimillions thereafter. It was all done by using the book in conjunction with radio.

Your book, your bestselling book, is your gateway to greater authority, celebrity, and client attraction. That's the good news.

The bad news? Well, let me tell you something. It's dang hard to write, publish, and promote a book, especially if you don't know what you're doing.

A few years ago, the *New York Times* did a survey and found that 81 percent of adult Americans wanted to write a book. Let me say it again, 81 percent! The *New York Times* actually thought that was a ridiculously high number, and, quite frankly, I do too. Not to worry though, because only about 1 percent ever follow through with completing it. What makes you and me special is not the desiring to do it but rather the doing itself.

You see, the model to write, publish, promote, and profit from a book has been hopelessly broken for years. This old model, which I not so favorably call Author 1.0 has prevented you from accomplishing your goal. If up until now you have not been able to get your book written, published, and marketed to bestseller, then don't be too concerned. There is a better way, an Author 2.0.

There are three primary elements to getting everything you want accomplished with a book. We call them Publish. Promote. Profit.™ and even trademarked the 2.0 process.

The original Publish 1.0 was everything you needed to actually get your book written and ready for market. In 1.0, this meant grinding daily over thousands of words, or going away to a cabin in the woods, often without a clear writing direction. Then hoping that an agent and a traditional publisher would grace you with favor and publish your work. Sounds horrible, because it is. No wonder people quit on it.

In Promote 1.0, you had to already have a large platform in place to market your book. To get a traditional publishing deal, you would be asked several questions that revolved around the size of your following and platform. You'd be asked about your email list, your social following (Facebook, LinkedIn, Instagram, Twitter), and your overall business. That's great, if you have a huge following and your name is Kim Kardashian or one of the housewives of Orange County. It's not so great, if you are an expert or entrepreneur too busy helping real people to Snapchat your latest meal.

And what about Profit 1.0? Well, you went through all that hell to make $1.62 per book that sells—royalties. The plan was to sell hundreds of thousands (or millions) and make bank. Sounds good, except, only a fraction of a percent of people ever do that.

So, like others before you, you do the math and ask, "Is this really worth it?" In fact, I am sitting on a plane right now on the way back from a speaking engagement in Montreal and during the Q&A that was the first question. Is it really worth it to write a book?

Look, authors are well-respected, because it is hard. Stay with me though, because in the pages that follow I will lay out your completely new, Author 2.0 plan that simplifies and shortcuts this process. Author 2.0 reduces your time and ensures that you have the absolute best chances for future success.

AUTHOR 1.0 vs. 2.0

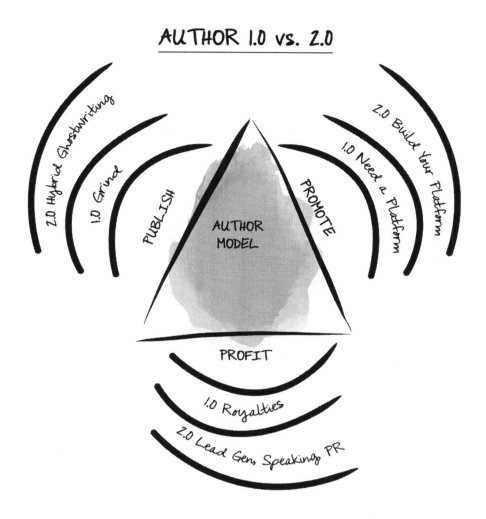

Author 1.0 vs 2.0 Model

A word of warning. The strategies outlined in this book are contrarian. Like the idea of me giving my book away on local radio. Many authors I share this idea with are repulsed at the idea of giving their book away. I think they hate money.

Much of this book is contrarian in nature, maybe because I am. But I prefer to be straightforward and tell you what is working right now for me and my clients, whether or not it is outside conventional thought. I'm pragmatic. To me, what works is what matters.

This might initially go against how you originally wanted to use your book. Perhaps you just hoped to publish your book and crowds would beat a path to your door. You know, in some cases, that actually happens, after all someone has to win the lottery, right?

Then again, this book is not about getting lucky. This book is for those who wish to be proactive, rather than reactive, with the use of their book. As the old saying goes, "I'd rather be lucky than good." Well, not me. I'd rather be good than lucky.

So, here's to getting good and making our own luck with our bestselling books.

Section One

Publish

CHAPTER 2

S'mores Anyone?
(Laying the Foundation)

"Art is about building a new foundation,
not just laying something on top of
what's already there."

—Prince

A few years ago, a construction company was building a new, three-story building next to my office in Pasadena. I was really amazed at two things. First, how deep a hole had to be dug to lay the foundation for a simple (relatively), three-story building. And second, how fast the building was built after the foundation was laid.

At BSP, we speak to potential authors every week. In fact, we receive over 500 applications to speak to us every single month. The biggest mistake that I hear is found in potential authors not laying the proper foundation prior to starting the writing process.

One specific conversation with a potential author was quite memorable. After the usual pleasantries, I asked why he wanted to write a book and what the goal of the book was. By the way, two important questions that you need to answer for yourself.

> I asked why he wanted to write a book and what the goal of the book was.

After some hemming and hawing and sharing how he has had an interesting life and wanted to write about that, he abruptly said, "Look, I've written over a thousand pages and I'm just wondering if you can help me."

My equally abrupt response was, "Yeah, I can come over and we can light it on fire and roast s'mores while discussing what you really want to write."

Yes, I really said that. Not my finest moment. A little harsh (and sarcastic) perhaps, but true nonetheless.

Now, I acknowledge that you might already have your book done or might be well on your way to finishing it. What I ask is that you try to leave some of your preconceived ideas about the topic of your book at the door, so we can discover together a truly solid foundation for your work.

To lay a solid foundation for your book, I'd like you to consider three things.

1. What is your specific goal or desired outcome for your book?

And don't say, I want to sell a million copies.

My first book built a multimillion-dollar business, led to major media and speaking opportunities, and even fostered two other million-dollar companies, and in 10 years I've sold *only* about 40,000 copies.

Douglas Bowman and John Mullen came to me in mid-2017, not long after an emotionally moving trip to Mozambique that changed their lives. Douglas and John experienced firsthand the devastation left by land mines on the people of Mozambique and vowed to do something about it.

They decided to start a charity and a movement with their book that tells the story of one particular person who touched their hearts. They wrote their book, *Florencia—An Accidental Story,* and we launched it in August 2017.

Today, almost one year later, *Florencia* remains a top 10 bestseller on Amazon. The men raised over $250,000 for their new charity in the first few months, using the book to bring attention and awareness.

They then used the book to get an introduction to the president of Mozambique. In one month, I am traveling with John and Douglas to speak to the General Assembly of the United Nations, where 200+ ambassadors to the United Nations will receive a copy of Doug and John's book.

All this, because their goal was to use the book to grow their charity and to start a movement that would make a difference in the lives of the people of Mozambique.

After all, how can you achieve success without begin crystal clear on your goal and desired outcome?

After all, how can you achieve success without begin crystal clear on your goal and desired outcome?

2. What is your audience's main problem or concern that you can solve?

If we don't recognize or understand our audience's problem, then how can we communicate our solution to their problem?

If we don't think about what our readers' needs are, what their difficulties are, and what their pains are, then we really can't communicate our value to them.

Without recognizing our audience, their challenges, their aspirations, and their desires, we can't communicate with them in a way that makes them take action.

3. What is the conversation going on in the readers' head, so that you can enter and "hook them"?

As a kid, I lived in Central Florida and used to go fishing a lot. The prize catch for me was the large-mouth bass.

Most bass anglers will use either worms or shiners of some kind, because those are most likely to produce results. Can you catch a bass on a bread ball? Uh, no. If you want to catch a bass, then you use the bait they are most likely to hit.

There is only one kind of fish in Central Florida that, literally, you could put anything on the hook and catch it. That is a gar or an alligator gar fish. In fact, it will bite a bare hook.

Now gar are known as "garbage fish," because they are not edible, and their snout looks like an alligator's. As you can imagine, it's not pleasant trying to remove a hook from their mouths.

You're asking, "Rob, who cares about fishing in Central Florida?" Well, not even me anymore, since I've taken up golf, but there is a point.

It's so important to understand that your book could literally lay the foundation for the next 10 or even 20 years of your life and business.

If you're trying to hook a specific fish, then you need a specific bait. Your bait is knowing what the needs are and communicating your solutions to those needs, in the words that the readers use.

It's so important to understand that your book could literally lay the foundation for the next 10 or even 20 years of your life and business.

On the heels of a devastating bankruptcy, Dave Ramsey wrote *Financial Peace: Restoring Financial Hope to You and Your Family*. That one book became the foundation for an information empire that is still going strong, more than 20 years later.

Did Dave plan that? I don't know, nor does it matter. As I said previously, I'd rather be good than lucky. And planning your book around these principles will give you the best chance of success and longevity with your topic.

The first question that your prospective reader asks is this.

Out of all the available options of books, products, or services, why should I read yours (as opposed to anybody else) or, in fact, why should I read anything at all?

That's a phrase I learned from Dan Kennedy.

Kennedy is the father of direct response marketing in recent times. Although he speaks about it in relation to people selling consulting or services, this question also applies to your audience and to selling books that then lead to sales of services, products, or coaching and consulting.

> So, out of all the available books on your particular topic, why should I read yours?

So, out of all the available books on your particular topic, why should I read yours? Why should I be attracted to your book, as opposed to another book or as opposed to not reading a book on the subject at all?

That's the first question that you want to ask as though you are your avatar (customer).

The first thing we have our clients do when they get started with BSP is fill out what we call our author market questionnaire. This questionnaire is a deep dive into the demographics and psychographics of our client's ideal audience or avatar.

We want to know the fears, frustrations, wants, and aspirations of our client's ideal customer. These details help us to brainstorm the hook, title, subtitle, and contents so we have a work that our client's audience resonates with and deeply hungers for.

Our (and Our Audience's) Desires Are Deeply Rooted

I'm in several mastermind groups that I invest a significant amount of money in to be a part of. These groups have furthered my business in more ways than I can count.

A few years ago, we had a highly successful tech investor in Silicon Valley do a session for a group of about 50 on understanding our customer avatar.

His previous success in Silicon Valley now allowed him to pursue his passion, which was about helping people to discover who they are and how they are meant to serve the world.

He asked us, "Who would like some help in digging deeper into whom their customer avatar is?" Of course, I eagerly volunteered. After all, what could go wrong, right?

He began, "OK, so you want to start going deeper into whom it is you're meant to serve?" (Which is a little different than "defining your customer avatar"!)

He said, "Great. Let's have a discussion. Do you feel comfortable discussing this in front of everybody?"

I said, "Well, yeah, of course." Why wouldn't I?

He continued, "All right, the first thing I want you to do is to get a pen and paper out. I want you to answer this question. I want you to tell me, what is your first, most traumatic childhood memory?"

I thought, *Wow, my most traumatic childhood memory? What in the world does that have to do with my customer avatar? And why in the world would I want to discuss that with you and 50 strangers.*

As you might imagine, things got a little uncomfortable for me at that point. Sharing my darkest childhood memory with 50 strangers.

The interesting thing is . . .

Though I had a fairly good childhood, I didn't grow up with my parents. I grew up with my grandparents and didn't know my mom. In fact, I didn't meet my mom until I turned 30 years old. So, as you might imagine, that became the topic.

His premise for me was that not knowing my mom had me constantly seeking attention from other sources (perhaps getting in trouble as a kid, hmmm) and looking for deeper meaning by being viewed as an authority.

I could certainly see the potential connection. When I discussed the specifics of my business, which is really about getting people attention and authority in their fields, then everyone had a light bulb moment.

His whole concept (and this is where we get to tie in the customer avatar part for you) is that the reason we aspire to certain things, the reason we go in a certain direction, is because there are deep yearnings within us.

These are deep needs within us that were formed from a childhood want, a traumatic memory, a difficulty, or something we might have experienced in childhood.

And here, based on my childhood memories, I've created this entire business all about helping people to get attention and become bestsellers, to get noticed and build their businesses.

> If you want a successful book, then start first with a foundation focused on the deep needs of your ideal client.

He was able to see a direct connection between what I do as my business and what I might have been lacking as a child.

And I actually thought we were going to talk about customer avatars.

Now whether my business and childhood are a direct correlation or only a loose association doesn't really matter. The point is that our desires are deeply rooted. They are not completely logic based, whether we realize that or not. The same is true of your ideal client.

If you want a successful book, then start first with a foundation focused on the deep needs of your ideal client.

CHAPTER 3

Lions, Tigers, and Bears? No—Titles, Subtitles, and Contents: Now That's Scary

"I'm writing a book. I've got the page numbers done."

—Steven Wright

There's a lot in a title.

When it comes to making judgments about people, we are admonished to never judge a book by its cover. Yet I can promise you that we are often judged by our "covers."

Similarly, books are judged and, more important, sold based on their covers and titles. Approach this topic lightly at your own (and your book's) peril.

Did you know that Russian author Leo Tolstoy's epic work *War and Peace* was originally titled *All's Well That Ends Well*? In fact, it was released under that title and did rather poorly initially until the title was changed.

American writer and actress Jacqueline Susann's *Valley of the Dolls* was originally titled *They Don't Build Statues to Businessmen*.

The Last Man in Europe was the original title for English novelist George Orwell's classic work, 1984.

Russian-American novelist Ayn Rand's famous book *Atlas Shrugged* was originally called *The Strike*, but Rand felt it gave away too much of the plot.

Even *Gone with the Wind*, written by American Margaret Mitchell, went through this with a working tile of *Tomorrow Is Another Day*, the book's iconic last line.

One of the greatest examples of this is American actress and writer Naura Hayden's book, originally titled *Astro-Logical Love*. When released under that title, the book fell completely flat.

Sometime later, Hayden took the same book, made minor changes to the content, but released it under a different title and cover. *How to Satisfy a Woman Every Time and Have Her Beg for More!* became a *New York Times* bestseller and affected a generation.

Take the time necessary to get this right.

There are three primary characteristics to a good book title—curiosity provoking, interesting, and memorable.

Malcolm Gladwell's books are a great example. Gladwell follows the same format in all his national bestsellers.

First, his main titles are one, two, or three words, and they offer a curiosity and interest to the reader. Three examples of Gladwell's better-known works are *Outliers*, *The Tipping Point*, and *Blink*.

The first impression of his title *Outliers* is interest and curiosity. You get the sense that you know what it is about but are interested in taking next steps at the same time, wondering, just what exactly he means.

Finding a word or short phrase for your topic and audience is pure gold. If you can find one, two, or three words that capture your reader's interest, and it provokes curiosity or emotion, then you have a winner.

Can you use four words in a title? Of course, you can. How about five or six? Yes. I am only using Gladwell's titles as an example, but a good one nonetheless.

To help with that, I'd like to recommend two books by Richard Bayan that I use: *Words That Sell: More than 6,000 Entries to Help You Promote Your Products, Services, and Ideas and More Words That Sell: A Thesaurus to Help You Promote Your Products, Services, and Ideas.* By the way, the titles of these books use the exact same framework that we're talking about

These books contain thousands of words that haven been studied. They can be used as a cross reference and guide for your research.

Next, we craft the subtitle.

Does your book absolutely need a subtitle? Well, if it's nonfiction, then more than likely it does. This also depends on your title. If your title is a short, curiosity-provoking one, like we have discussed above, then almost certainly it will need a subtitle to give further explanation and benefit to the reader.

The subtitle is your descriptive, benefit-rich, wording that explains the promise of the book.

> The subtitle is your descriptive, benefit-rich, wording that explains the promise of the book.

Going back to Gladwell, for example purposes, he uses short subtitles that give an explanation as to the content of the book, such as *The Tipping Point: How Little Things Can Make a Big Difference, Outliers: The Story of Success*, or *Blink: The Power of Thinking without Thinking.*

So, the subtitle is more descriptive and benefit-rich, expressing the promise of the book.

The best way for you to approach this is to take some time and make a benefits list, which consists of 7–10 benefits of your solution to your ideal prospect's problem. Or, thought of another way, the benefits that someone will get from reading your book.

For example, take Timothy Ferris' book, *The Four-Hour Workweek: Escape 9–5, Live Anywhere, and Join the New Rich.* The clear benefits of reading his book are spelled out in the subtitle. His ideal reader (and client) is interested in escaping the 9–5 workday, living anywhere they want, and being rich.

As a sidenote, the human mind often thinks comfortably in ones and threes. I would recommend you use either one clear benefit (like Gladwell does) or three benefits, like Ferris does. His book title offers three clear benefits for reading the book.

Even if your book is already complete, you can still make adjustments to your title so that you hook your ideal audience.

Developing Your Contents Page

There are many ways for you to lay out your contents page, but for our purposes I am going to give you the three that we focus on the most.

They are logical order of progression, segmentation by content, and nonsequential questioning.

Logical Order of Progression

This is the simplest and easiest to implement. A good example of this is found in a book I recently read: *Principles: Life and Work* by Ray Dalio. His book is Amazon's 2017 business book of the year and I highly recommend it.

(I am often asked what my favorite book is. Though it might seem like a copout, it is typically the book I am currently reading.)

Dalio's book is divided into two parts, and part one is a perfect example of this logical order of progression. In part one, there are eight chapters, and they simply progress through his life from 1949 to the present.

1. My Call to Adventure: 1949–1967
2. Crossing the Threshold: 1967–1979
3. My Abyss: 1979–1982
4. My Road of Trials: 1983–1994
5. The Ultimate Boon: 1995–2010
6. Returning the Boon: 2011–2015
7. My Last Year and My Greatest Challenge: 2016–2017
8. Looking Back from a Higher Level

A word of warning. Ray Dalio is a billionaire and grew the largest hedge fund in the world. I hardly think anyone, other than my own children (and perhaps not them), would be interested in such a book from me. In my opinion, you should also take such a stance. Unless, of course, you too are a self-made, world-famous billionaire.

Always make the book, chapters, and content about your ideal clients—their problems, concerns, and desires. Fit your story into that, and logical progression will work for you.

Segmentation by Content

Next is what I refer to as segmentation by content. A great example of segmentation by content can be found by looking at one of the best business books of all time: *The Seven Habits of Highly Effective People* by Stephen Covey.

Always make the book, chapters, and content about your ideal clients— their problems, concerns, and desires.

When you look at the contents page, you can see that it's segmented into four parts. There isn't necessarily a logical progression to the content.

You might ask why that is necessary. In this case, Covey had to explain seven particular habits that don't necessarily build directly upon another habit sequentially.

Because the habits can be mutually exclusive from one another, Covey has four parts to his contents page. Each of these are segmented by the content or type of habit in his case.

In the first segment, "Part One: Paradigms and Principles," Covey lays the foundation for the rest of the book. It is an overview and introduction to everything he is going to follow with.

"Part Two: Private Victory" has three habits segmented in the section. Habit one is "Be Proactive—Principles of Personal Vision." Habit two is "Begin with the End in Mind—Principles of Personal Leadership."

Habit three is "Put First Things First—Principles of Personal Management."

These are all principles of "private victory," and the chapters are based on what Covey thought were the three key habits that had the most to do with private victory.

"Part Three: Public Victory" includes habit four, "Think Win/ Win—Principles of Interpersonal Leadership"; habit five, "Seek First to Understand, Then to Be Understood—Principles of Empathic Communication; and habit six, "Synergize—Principles of Creative Cooperation."

"Part Four: Renewal" covers habit seven, "Sharpen the Saw—Principles of Balanced Self-Renewal" and a conclusion titled "Inside-Out Again."

You can see that there are basically seven chapters, but they're segmented into these four different sections, with one not needed to build on another.

If you are writing a book with principles that don't necessarily build upon one another but rather fit neatly in sections, then this is a nice format for your work. It enables you to create a nice flow for your content, just like Stephen Covey did with this classic book.

Segmentation by content is the second way you can create your contents page.

Nonsequential Questioning

The third way to create your contents page is what I call nonsequential questioning.

Nonsequential questioning is best when you have a book that answers questions (or deals with principles or challenges that someone might be facing) that don't have any natural sequence. The goal is to address the questions in whatever sequence you choose, without parts or sections, because they do not naturally fit together.

Our client Robert Szentes' book is a good example of this. His book is titled *The Mastering of Your Mind—Forever Change Your Destructive Beliefs to Break Free from Your Past Limitations and Live the Life of Your Dreams.*

Robert's book did well, and it became a number-one, national bestseller.

His book consists of an introduction, nine chapters, a conclusion, acknowledgments, and an about-the-author page.

Robert lays the foundation of his book in the beginning, with chapter one, "Our Mind and Our Beliefs—Limiting Belief Fundamentals."

Chapter two is "Why We Block Out the Good—Not Feeling Deserving and Worthy" and begins what he considers the seven, big, limiting beliefs that people have.

Chapter three is "There Is Not Enough—Scarcity Mindset."

Chapter four is "I Am Alone—The Fear of Being Alone."

Chapter five is "Secrets to Lasting Self-Esteem."

Chapter six is "Our Power and Strength."

Chapter seven is "Stuck in Our Deepest Fears."

As you can see, there is no natural sequence or order to Robert's book, because one limiting belief does not necessarily occur with another.

These limiting beliefs are then addressed one by one and not included in any section or part.

This is what we call nonsequential questioning and might be a good fit for your book, if it meets the criteria discussed previously.

Layout Out Your Contents Page

Just to be clear, there's no right or wrong way to create your contents page. You don't have to strictly adhere to any one method outlined here, and you can certainly mix and match, as needed. My goal is to help you get unstuck and have some format in mind as you create your contents page. These three ideas are all examples of ways you can add some flair and creativity to your story and your expertise.

Remember, if you want a successful book, then start first with a foundation focused on the deep needs of your ideal client.

CHAPTER 4

The Problem with Writing Is the Writing

"Easy reading is damn
hard writing."

—**Nathaniel Hawthorne**

There's a big problem that no one talks about when it comes to content creation. It's dang hard!

I remember when attorney Delano Lewis first came to me to get help with his book. I was excited to potentially be working with the former US ambassador to South Africa, a gentleman in his early 70s, who not only had reached the heights of the political world, working directly with revolutionary Nelson Mandela and in the Bill Clinton presidential administration, but he also was the former CEO of National Public Radio (NPR), and had sat on the board of the Colgate-Palmolive Company for over 20 years.

Here was this incredibly successful man in every area of his life, and yet he told me that he had been trying to write his book for over 10 years.

He was interested in getting on the speaking circuit and starting the third iteration of his business life, speaking at colleges and universities about his experiences and inspiring the youth of today.

He had worked with a traditional ghostwriter and gotten poor results. He also tried to write on his own but was unhappy with the lack of flow. He began to wonder if he would ever get this accomplished.

The standard way of writing a book, grinding it out or perhaps using a traditional ghostwriter, were both things that he had tried and had been unsuccessful with. If they did not help him attain success with his book, then really, how could anybody?

In speaking to thousands of successful entrepreneurs who are attempting to write a book, I've learned a few things. Most people think that there are only those two ways to get the content for their book created.

The first thought is usually to grind it out by writing 500–1,000 words every day (something taught by many gurus, by the way). It's a great idea, but few actually do it.

Or perhaps go away on a personal nature retreat (which didn't work out too well in *The Shining*—just saying) to finally get your book done.

And if those don't work, then the other option is to hire a traditional ghostwriter. This was the option I chose when writing my first book, because I knew myself well enough to know I would not write every day.

I mentioned earlier that I had made many mistakes in the creation process of my first book. Well, my first and really most costly mistake in getting my book done was made in hiring a traditional ghostwriter.

Knowing that I wasn't going to create my book by writing 1,000 words per day and also that I really needed to get this book done as quickly as possible meant my options were limited. I needed to position myself better in the marketplace for my new business, and my book was going to be the primary tool for me to do that. Every day counted.

So, I pulled the trigger and hired a traditional ghostwriter.

The first step with most traditional ghostwriters is in preparing the title, subtitle, and contents page. The more expensive writers ($25,000+) will typically assist in this process. This was really no problem for me, because I had a marketing background and understood the need to niche my subject and create a hook. This was done quickly, and we were off.

> I needed to position myself better in the marketplace for my new business, and my book was going to be the primary tool for me to do that.

After this, we began our content creation. Traditionally, ghostwriters will have one-on-one, question-and-answer times with you about a chapter's content. Then, when they are satisfied there is enough material, they move on to the next chapter until all the content is recorded.

We followed that exact procedure. After many hours of recording over a period of about two to three months, we finished. I was so excited the day she told me we had enough material for her to begin writing. We were almost there. Yeah, right!

I still remember when I got the rough draft delivered to me. *Rough draft, so that's why they call it that*, I thought. As I started to go through the text, I immediately knew there was a major problem.

I read through the introduction, and I didn't like it. I read through the first chapter, and I liked it less.. By the time I got finished with the third chapter, I knew we had a real issue.

Why? What was it about the book that I hated so much? Was it the sentence structure or the grammar of the writer? No, absolutely not. Her sentence structure, grammar, and punctuation were far better than mine.

What was the problem then? The problem was that the book was not in my voice. It didn't sound anything like me. It didn't have my characteristics, personality, or quirks in it at all. After looking at it for several weeks, I realized there was no way to save it.

I ended up throwing it away and then taking the next eight months to write my book myself. I said this was the costliest mistake that I'd made. To be clear, the cost was not in what I paid the ghostwriter, though that was a lot of money. The expense was that this ended up costing me one year of work and effort without getting my book completed.

The first year after I got my book done with my business, I did over a million dollars in revenue.

As I've said to you before, the first year after I got my book done with my business, I did over a million dollars in revenue. If I would've had my book completed and gotten a year's headstart, I would've made an extra million dollars. By far, my most costly mistake.

I came to learn that this is a common problem with traditional ghostwriting.

So how do we solve this?

I thought if I could find a way to have the best of both worlds, then we'd have something special. The goal became to have an expert writer craft a well-written work and, at the same time, it would also be in the author's voice.

Hybrid ghostwriting was born.

The basic premise of the hybrid ghostwriting process is that you speak your book, but you do it in a presentation-style format that enables the writer to capture the voice of the author. You can also choose to do this on your own, but because the spoken word tends to be different than the written word, you will need to edit or rewrite it yourself or have someone else do it.

So, what is this presentation-style format I speak of? Glad you asked. Have you ever seen a great TED or TEDx Talk?

If not, go to Ted.com right now and watch one. They are compelling, interesting, informative, and short—from 5 to 18 minutes. This is exactly how you should create your chapter content.

The best TED or TEDx Talks are all similar in style. They start with a compelling story that leaves the audience hanging on every word and often, though not always, also contain an open loop. The speaker then discusses the main points of his or her talk, using elements of the story to illustrate them. Then culminates the talk with conclusion of the story or perhaps another story that makes the point more powerful.

Simple and elegant.

It was an epiphany for me to realize that I (and my clients) could create compelling content in this exact format that makes the audience beg for more.

When it comes time for our clients to start their hybrid ghostwriting process, we explain this process to them. We tell them that we want them to treat each chapter recording as though they're giving an 18-minute presentation (TED Talk) to an audience of their ideal clients.

And if you were to give a presentation like this, to 10 or 100 of your ideal clients, there are certain elements of your presentation that you want to be really clear on.

So, if you're going to be presenting on content from chapter one of your material, then what we want you to do is come up with a three-point lesson (more or less is OK too). These are the three or so major points that you want to focus on in that particular chapter.

You will want to come up with one or two stories that hook your audience and that also illustrate the main points you're making in this chapter's content.

And then, we want you to end with a bang, so that it's memorable. So, perhaps you end with a memorable quote or perhaps (just as you would when ending a live presentation) you find a way to end it powerfully by culminating the story.

> It's in your voice, it's highlighting your passion, and it's your particular content.

What makes the hybrid ghostwriting process really simple and easy is that it's in your voice, it's highlighting your passion, and it's your particular content, presented with your stories and your examples that make it come alive and exciting!

It's not just facts and statistics, it's you and your personality that make it really interesting.

Three Key Elements of the Hybrid Ghostwriting Process

There are three key elements to consider when you implement the hybrid ghostwriting process.

1. Story

First, you want to start with story.

We all love stories. People might initially come to you or your book because of your knowledge or expertise, but they will only stay (and read) if you have compelling stories.

Your chapter opening stories should be complete with ups and downs, challenges, pitfalls, and overcoming adversity. Ideally, you would want to use case studies from clients, in addition to stories from your personal life. You will want to start with a story in every chapter. And they don't have to all be your stories, either.

If you have certain points to make and do not have a case study or personal story that represents it, well, then don't worry. The stories can be from history, they can be stories from sports, they can be great analogies, they can be anything that you find that is gripping and leads into the content that you want to share.

Remember, the main way to grip the audience, right from the beginning, is story.

2. Content

The second element is having great content.

It's not enough to just start with a great story. You want to start with a great story that then flows perfectly into the point or points that you want to make about that chapter's content.

Usually, content is not the most challenging part of the creation process. Obviously, you are an expert in your space and have much to teach and convey about the topic.

Imagine, for a moment, beginning your chapter with a harrowing tale of failure or near calamity. Sharing all the forces set against you and the uncertainty of success. Yet, at the same time, the reader knows that you got out of that and appeared successfully on the other side.

However, imagine that instead of simply sharing the entire story of failure to success, you stop at the point of greatest uncertainty and fear. This is called an open loop. Because of how our brains work, the reader is compelled to read more and find out the conclusion of the story.

Great structure is necessary to compel the reader to continue and to learn, while being entertained in the process.

Instead of concluding the story at this point, you begin to share the lessons learned in the process—your content. The ways you coped or changes you made in midstream that ultimately changed your course.

The readers now begin to form their own conclusions and learn from your story, while being gripped and compelled to read more.

Great structure is necessary to compel the reader to continue and to learn, while being entertained in the process.

3. Close

Last, you want to end strong.

Remember that every chapter is kind of a microcosm of your whole book. Every chapter has to hook the readers, interest them, and give them great content and information. Then it has to end with something that is memorable and strong.

So, how do you do that?

The easiest way is to conclude the story that you left them hanging on during the open loop. In some cases, though, there is a need for an additional story to add strength to your argument and make the conclusion more powerful.

Remember, think in terms of a speaking engagement. If you're standing in front of an audience, and you've had them hanging on every word, then you won't want to let them down now with a poor conclusion. I tell my authors that their stories and how they're told are often the hardest part of the writing process. So, take your time here, and make sure that you have the elements in place for success.

These three parts are simple, but they're important. When you do this right for each chapter, it becomes simple to create a presentation that's just 20 or 25 minutes long and has all the elements of an amazing chapter.

You start with story, you continue with great structure, and then you end with a strong conclusion. That's the hybrid ghostwriting process and, though simple, it's powerful.

Would you like a bonus? There is one more thing that is not present in TED Talks but absolutely should be present in your chapters content. That is, "what's next?"

You see, while a book is an amazing way to engage readers, it is a one-sided conversation. They are reading your words, but you have no way to communicate with them. I direct all our authors to provide additional content and next steps for readers to drive them from your book to your website and your email list, so you can begin actively communicating with them.

So, consider at the end of every chapter how you can create an additional resource, cheat sheet, video, tip sheet, or the like, that will add value to the readers' experience and connect them to you with joy to get your next thing. Don't finish a chapter without next steps.

Oh, by the way, former US Ambassador Delano Lewis is now an international bestseller, featured by our public relations (PR) team on six different TV shows and is currently speaking on stages and universities across America. That's called closing the loop.

> Consider at the end of every chapter how you can create an additional resource... that will add value to the readers' experience...

To see what Delano Lewis had to say about the process, go to https://go.bestsellerpublishing.org/delano. That's your next step.

Section Two

Promote

CHAPTER 5

Rocket Man (or Woman) Book Launch Success

> "I wrote a best-selling book, and if you don't believe me, you can come into my basement; I'll show you every copy."
>
> **—Anthony Scaramucci**

I expect this will be one of the more popular and useful sections of this book.

"Why?" you might ask.

Well, simply stated I know the facts about book sales and, unfortunately, they are quite dreary.

The good news is that with the rise of Amazon, it is easier than ever to publish your book. The bad news is that with the rise of Amazon, it is easier than ever to publish a book. There is so much noise in the marketplace. So many books and marketing messages and so little time.

A simple search on Amazon for almost any topic will illustrate the point. There are far more failures than successes. Books that are poorly published and even more poorly marketed (but perhaps well written?) tend to be complete failures for the author. Heck, even well-written and published books tend to be failures, if they are not marketed properly.

There is so much noise in the marketplace. So many books and marketing messages and so little time.

You can easily see this by the number of reviews on a book in addition to its status in competition with other books in its category.

I remember when Ted Kallman and Andrew Kallman first came to me after writing their beautifully done book *The Nehemiah Effect: Ancient Wisdom from the World's First Agile Projects*. It was incredibly well crafted, the cover was nicely done, the title was catchy, and these guys were cold-stone experts at their craft.

The challenge was it was in an extremely narrow category.

You see Ted and Andrew are agile consultants, primarily to manufacturing firms. This, in and of itself, is a tiny sliver of a small category. Ted and Andrew were smart though and had a great plan for the marketing of their book.

Sadly most authors simply publish their book and cross their fingers, hoping that it will catch fire. You see, one of the statistics that is never discussed is that the average book sells about 250 copies in its lifetime.

Imagine pouring your blood, sweat, and tears into your life's work and only a couple of hundred people ever buy it. The truth is actually worse than that. Of the 250 people who purchase, most are sold to the author and the author's friends and family. Thanks, Mom and Dad!

Some time back, we got a call at BSP from a traditionally published author asking for marketing help from our team. It's rather common actually. Come to find out, what he wanted help with was selling the 8,000 books in his garage that the publisher made him buy. I nicely declined. Like the Scaramucci quote, many authors of traditional publishing houses are under contract to buy thousands of books that sit in their garages, basements, or warehouses for years. They never tell you that when you're after the big advance though.

When it comes to your book marketing, the image that needs to come to mind to you is that of the Space Shuttle launches from the 1980s. I'm not a rocket scientist (though I do play one on television from time to time) but my understanding is that the Space Shuttle, which sat on top of a giant fuel tank with two giant rocket boosters on each side of it, would use about 90 percent or more of its fuel just to get out of Earth's atmosphere. Once it got out of the atmosphere, the giant fuel tank and the rocket boosters would fall off, and the Space Shuttle could travel faster and faster using little fuel.

You see, your book marketing must follow the exact same process. There are 4,000 marketing messages a day hitting your ideal client. There will be a million-plus books published this year on Amazon, and for your book to be noticed, you're going to have to make it stand out with your marketing and with your launch process.

This was the same challenge that Andrew and Ted faced, and they contacted BSP wo help with the launch process.

So, we decided to do a full, book-launch strategy, which we will be covering in great detail in this section. Yes, you can relaunch a book, if at first the book did not sell successfully. Fix what is broken and push the button.

There are five key elements we will be discussing in the book launch phase.

1. Book cover and design elements
2. Reviews
3. Press releases
4. Free and paid advertising
5. Social media strategy

We've launched over 400 bestsellers for our clients, and each one goes through the exact same five-step process.

We've launched over 400 bestsellers for our clients, and each one goes through the exact same five-step process.

Image of Books from Our Banner

Ted and Andrew's launch went through the five-step process and was incredibly successful. *The Nehemiah Effect* became a bestselling book in multiple categories and in multiple countries.

The Nehemiah Effect remained number one, over a period of about seven months, in Amazon's consulting category.

From the success of the launch, they got many speaking engagement opportunities and new clients. I received a beautiful Facebook message from them on Christmas Eve 2014, expressing their successes.

They shared that just one consulting client from the launch had accounted for $80,000 in revenue to their business. In fact, from the launch of the book, they did over $250,000 in income, got multiple speaking engagements, and watched their business explode, all because the book was launched properly.

Even more exciting was that they got a one-on-one meeting with the CEO of a traditional publishing company. Because of the success of their book after the launch that we did, they received a large book advance for their next book, which they're currently in the process of writing.

Perhaps you've already written a book and have been discouraged with the results it received. Follow this process and watch your book lift off!

To learn whether or not your book would qualify for BSP's book launch process, go to http://go.bestsellerpublishing.org/get-started

CHAPTER 6

The 800-Pound Gorilla

"It's a little like wrestling a gorilla. You don't quit when you're tired—you quit when the gorilla is tired."

—**Robert Strauss**

In 2014, a quiet war broke out between traditional publishers and Amazon. Amazon was controlling (at that time) approximately 65 percent of the ebook market share and desiring to lower the barrier of entry and prices and capture even more of the market. Traditional publishers fought to protect their ebook cash cow and keep the barrier of entry high.

So, what happened?

Depends on whom you ask, but today, in 2018, Amazon controls about 83 percent of the US market, which accounts for a staggering 1,000,000 paid ebook downloads per day. Yes, I said *per day*.

Today, Amazon controls a greater market share of sales than it did four years ago and continues to grow at a breakneck pace. Oh, and Jeff Bezos is the richest man in the world.

The 800-pound gorilla of the book publishing world is Amazon's Kindle Direct Publishing (KDP) program.

We will primarily be focused on the ebook version of your book for the book launch process. After the launch, you will also organically experience sales of both ebook and softcover or hardcover versions, but for the launch process we are primarily concerned with digital.

> Amazon's KDP program allows you to publish your book and reach millions of readers.

Amazon's KDP program allows you to publish your book as an ebook (for Amazon Kindle or the Kindle app) and reach millions of readers.

You can publish your Kindle ebook in less than five minutes, and your book appears on Kindle stores worldwide within 24–48 hours.

You can also earn up to 70 percent royalty on sales to customers in the US, Canada, UK, Germany, India, France, Italy, Spain, Japan, Brazil, Mexico, Australia, and more.

And, just as important, you keep control of your publishing rights and set your own list prices. You can also make changes to your books at any time.

So, this is how we're going to work to gain bestseller status—by publishing on the Kindle Direct Publishing platform!

Let's first take a look at our primary strategy of using the KDP Select five-day promo launch.

There are five steps in the KDP setup phase.

1. KDP upload
2. Amazon book description

3. Choosing categories
4. Verified reviews
5. Launch pricing strategy

KDP Upload

Amazon requires you to upload your ebook at least 24 hours prior to a KDP promotion, however, we would never recommend such procrastination. Plan on uploading your ebook a full two weeks prior to your scheduled promotion for several key reasons.

First, we want to make absolutely sure that the formatting and design is the highest quality. I can tell you many client horror stories, but rest assured that you do not want to send a ton of traffic from press releases, paid ads, and social media unless the formatting is right. People on the internet can be mean! Bad formatting means loads of one-star reviews, so get this right.

Second, we will be focused on getting as many four-star and five-star Amazon verified reviews during this time. An Amazon verified review is simply a review from someone who actually paid (.99 or greater) for your book. I'll be discussing our review strategies in the next section. This gives us two full weeks to go over our list, social media followers, and sphere of influence to get as many reviews as possible.

As a sidenote, one of our other goals will be to hit *hot new release* and *top-rated book* in our Amazon categories. We have to hit those within the first 30 days of uploading it into KDP. Hitting those gives us additional exposure on Amazon's platform.

Amazon Book Description

Your Amazon book description is often overlooked and rushed through by many authors, but I would caution against that. This is your opportunity to sell your book to prospective buyers, and it is also Amazon's way of determining who it should send to your book page. Amazon is primarily a gigantic buyer search engine and, similar to Google, you must have content on your book page that informs Amazon's algorithm who it should send your way.

Here are three ideas to focus on.

- Write the description as an advertisement with a compelling and catchy headline and first sentence.

- Write in the third person rather than directly from the author when talking about the merits of your book.

- Use keywords that Amazon will be able to use for search reference.

I always like to see examples of good work, so here is an example of a well-written description.

This is the description from Tony Robbins bestselling book, *Unshakeable: Your Financial Freedom Playbook*.

After interviewing fifty of the world's greatest financial minds and penning the #1 New York Times bestseller Money: *Master the Game, Tony Robbins returns with a step-by-step playbook, taking you on a journey to transform your financial life and accelerate your path to financial freedom. No matter your salary, your stage of life, or when you started, this book will provide the tools to help you achieve your financial goals more rapidly than you ever thought possible.*

Robbins, who has coached more than fifty million people from 100 countries, is the world's #1 life and business strategist. In this book, he teams up with Peter Mallouk, the only man in history to be ranked the #1 financial advisor in the US for three consecutive years by Barron's. Together they reveal how to become unshakeable—someone who can not only maintain true peace of mind in a world of immense uncertainty, economic volatility, and unprecedented change, but who can profit from the fear that immobilizes so many.

In these pages, through plain English and inspiring stories, you'll discover . . .

- *How to put together a simple, actionable plan that will deliver true financial freedom.*

- *Strategies from the world's top investors on how to protect yourself and your family and maximize profit from the inevitable crashes and corrections to come.*

- *How a few simple steps can add a decade or more of additional retirement income by discovering what your 401(k) provider doesn't want you to know.*

- *The core four principles that most of the world's greatest financial minds utilize so that you can maximize upside and minimize downside.*

- *The fastest way to put money back in your pocket: uncover the hidden fees and half truths of Wall Street—how the biggest firms keep you overpaying for underperformance.*

- *Master the mindset of true wealth and experience the fulfillment you deserve today.*

Choosing Categories

When uploading your book, you will be asked to choose two categories that match your book's content. Amazon has hundreds of categories and while it is fairly straightforward, there can be some discrepancies.

Some experts suggest choosing the most obscure and minor categories possible to give yourself the best chance to hit number one on Amazon. While I don't subscribe to placing your book in the underwater basket weaving category, I do suggest that you stay away from the most general categories. Focus instead on really choosing a category that defines your book's content.

Review these suggestions from the Amazon KDP page on how to choose categories.

- *Be accurate. Choose the most accurate categories based on the subject matter of your book. Avoid choosing one category that's explicitly fiction and another that's explicitly non-fiction. For example, if your book is a romance novel set during the U.S. Civil War, choose "Fiction > Romance > Historical." Do not include "History > US > Civil War." Instead, "US Civil War" as a keyword.*

- *Be specific. Choose specific categories instead of general ones. Customers looking for specific topics will find your book more easily. We'll display your book in the general categories as well. For example, a book in the "FICTION > Fantasy > Historical" category will also show up in searches for general fiction and general fantasy. Choose a "General" category only if your book is a general book about a broad topic.*

- *Don't be redundant. Choosing a single category will display your book in a variety of searches, so don't list your book in a category and its sub-categories. For example, don't select "FICTION > Fantasy > Historical" and "FICTION > Fantasy." One specific, accurate category is more effective than a redundant second one.*

- **Find examples.** *To find out which categories are the best fit for your book, search for categories on Amazon. For example, look for relevant browse categories on the left under the Kindle Store > Kindle eBooks header. You can also search for books like yours and find the browse categories assigned to those books. To do so, scroll down the book's detail page to the section "Look for Similar Items by Category."*

Verified Reviews

During the two-week period from the time we uploaded the book to the actual hard launch/promo date, we want to focus our attention on getting as many Amazon verified reviews for our book as possible. We recommend a minimum of five to seven reviews, but with a little bit of elbow grease, you can accomplish far more.

To clarify again, an Amazon verified review is a review from someone who actually purchased the book for at least .99 or more. This holds more weight with Amazon when it comes to Amazon's search algorithm.

It is recommended we keep the price at .99 to make it as painless as possible for our clients, followers, and friends to download the book and offer a review on it.

If you have a large follower base, then sending emails about the review period and low price in addition to posting on social media will experience amazing results.

Our client Kaelin Tuell Poulin, of www.ladyboss.com, got over 300 four-star and five-star reviews following our process.

Our client Jay Campbell, of www.totrevolution.com, got over 200 five-star reviews following the same process.

Your email, post, or direct outreach should have several elements in it.

1. Announcement of your new book and information that you are letting only your friends, family, and followers know right now because of the reduced ebook price that is temporary for the next two weeks.

2. Request that they download the ebook now for the reduced price of .99, and ask them to kindly offer you an honest review of the book on Amazon.

3. Suggest that they choose only two or three chapters to read and offer a review on the content of those chapters. This is because most people will not read the entire book and will feel that it is necessary for them to do so before they offer a review. Take that pressure off them and watch your reviews skyrocket.

Follow these guidelines, and in two weeks you will see great results.

Launch Pricing Strategy

Up until this point, our book has been priced at .99 and we have been focused on getting as many Amazon verified reviews as possible.

Now we shift into launch mode with our five-day KDP promotion.

Day before Launch

The day before the launch, we're going to raise our price for that one day ($9.99 prior to the five-day promo launch).

Why do we do this? There are many websites that make their followers aware of Kindle books that suddenly have a large price reduction.

These websites are set up to automatically alert the website subscribers about books that have been discounted.

So, when you raise your price to $9.99 and then, immediately the next day (or let's say two days later) your book is under the five-day free promo period, then you'll have many, many websites being alerted and notified of your book going on special—from almost $10 to free for five days!

Besides all the paid traffic and advertising that we do for our clients, we also make sure to promote it on any additional book-selling sites that are geared to offering discounted offers.

So, we'll raise the price for one day or sometimes two days to take advantage of those sites that are looking for discounted books.

Five-Day Promo Period

The five-day promotions we run for our clients start on Monday and run through Friday, with Friday being the fifth day. We do this because our company hours are Monday to Friday nine a.m. to five p.m., and we want to be able to monitor our clients' launches continually.

With that said, it is worthwhile for you to set your five-day promo around your schedule and what fits for you. Weekends are great times to sell books and ending the promotion on a weekend is a great idea. The primary suggestion I have is to end the promotion on either a Friday, Saturday, or Sunday due to buyer trends and habits.

End the Promo Early

We always suggest that you end your promo halfway through the final (fifth) day.

For example, BSP is in California, so we would end it at about noon on day five and we'd then price it at 99¢ for one week. There are a couple of reasons for this.

We're going to be driving an enormous amount of traffic to the book on days one through five and then, on day five, we issue another press release to hit and also create advertising that hits.

Because of this, people are going to be looking for a promo of the book. If the book is now at 99¢, in many cases it's not going to matter to them. If they're already interested in the book and they've already gone to the site for that, then we're going to get some downloads and get featured by Amazon (oftentimes as a hot new release or a top-rated book) simply by ending early on day five and keeping our price at 99¢ to get all that final promo-day traffic as purchases.

Raise Price to Full Retail

Finally, we want to raise our price to the full retail price we've decided on. We recommend somewhere between $2.99 and $9.99 for the digital version, while the softcover book should be priced between $19.95 and $24.95 from the beginning.

Now, someone might say, "Well, gosh! I'm going to lose all that money if someone buys the digital version." And that's true, but we're not really interested in making money during the launch period.

What we are interested in is getting the book as much attention as possible, making the book a bestseller, getting it to the hot new release section and making it a top-rated book. In other words, getting Amazon's attention!

And don't worry—the higher priced sales will come, down the road. Remember this is *only* for five days.

CHAPTER 7

Launch Party

> "There are no traffic jams
> on the extra mile."
>
> —Zig Ziglar

You've probably heard the term vicious cycle. It's the idea that things tend to go from bad to worse. In business, it might mean that you don't have enough money to market and advertise. Because you can't market, you're not generating enough leads, which means you're not generating the sales that you need. This leads to the vicious cycle, again, of not having enough money to market and to advertise. Not fun.

One of my clients, Bill Stack, coined the phrase virtuous cycle, which we greatly prefer. We helped Bill to write and market his book, *The 7.0 Percent Solution: Guaranteed Growth in a 0.7 Percent World*, to help him grow his financial advisory business. The book became an international bestseller in multiple categories, and we helped Bill be featured in major media all around the US. Over a period of just a few months, Bill was featured in *US News and World Report* twice. He was featured in Jim Cramer's *TheStreet* and also in *Reader's Digest*.

Not long after this, a large financial publication reached out to Bill, after seeing his book and his features in these publications, and asked if he would be a regular contributor to its financial magazine. To sweeten the pot, not only did the publication want him to be a regular contributor, but it was willing to pay him for his articles and said that he could promote himself, his book, and his services at the same time. This is when Bill called me and started to describe the virtuous cycle that his book had helped him create.

Bill's been in a professional organization for over 15 years for his financial advisory business, and he shared with me that in the first 14 years, though he did receive referrals, he was fairly unknown. In the past 12 months, all this has changed. In the past year, several executives of this professional organization heard about Bill's book and featured articles and they asked if they could feature his book in their professional library. Bill's book quickly became the number-one book in the entire professional library of this organization.

Three months after, they asked Bill to join the board of advisors, and just recently, Bill became the chair of the board of this professional organization. In the past year, Bill has gone from completely unknown and invisible to the chair of the board of this organization. The virtuous cycle has continued for Bill. Here's Bill's latest correspondence to me in our private client group.

> Sometimes we have to share the good with the bad. I don't want to spread bad vibes here, but BSP recently cost us $235 we otherwise may not have had to pay, had we not been involved with them. We paid for our book over a year ago, but unknown costs keep coming.
>
> Apparently, some retiring executives from out of state had seen our book, and wanted to hire me as their consultant. Cost $235 for registration/licensing in their state.
>
> While we did **receive over $37,000 to work with them**, we were still out the $235.

Just another one of those unknown/unmentioned costs, that comes with being a bestselling author with BSP.

Thanks again, Rob and staff!!

Bill has a wry sense of humor. And a virtuous cycle that continues.

The beginning of the virtuous cycle is always traffic—letting people know about you and your book. I tell my clients that there are only four reasons people do not buy from you.

> The beginning of the virtuous cycle is always traffic—letting people know about you and your book.

1. They don't know you exist.
2. They don't know if they can trust you.
3. They don't know if your magic works.
4. They don't believe in themselves.

From my experience, the first reason is always the biggest issue. Your book launch is your first step in dealing with the problem.

Your book launch consists of five main components.

1. Book cover and design elements
2. Reviews (see information that was covered in Chapter 6)
3. Press releases
4. Free and paid advertising
5. Social media strategy

Book Cover and Design Elements

Whether we like it or not, our book will be judged first by its cover. Often, books will be purchased based on the cover alone.

So, we need to really make sure that we're not spending years writing (if you've not followed my process) our heart and soul of material into our book and then get quick and cheap when it comes to the cover. Your audience might never get to the heart and soul of your material if the cover is not attractive.

> Your book will be judged first by its cover.

Cover Considerations

Here are five things to consider, when it comes to creating your cover design.

1. Put Yourself in Your Audience's Shoes

We discussed, in the foundation stage, the importance of intimately knowing your audience.

Of course, that's important for both your title and book cover, because you're going to speak to a 20-year-old female college student differently than you're going to speak to a 55-year-old male financial planner.

This is true not only for the wording that you use, but there can be differences in the colors and the imagery you use. So, first and foremost, know your audience and put yourself in their shoes.

Do your homework, research. Check to see if there are commonalities when it comes to cover imagery, colors used, or wording. (Not that you're going to knock anybody off, but if there is a theme across the demographic, then you want to follow that theme.)

2. Use Uncommon Words and Themes

A great example of this Malcolm Gladwell's classic book, *Outliers*. Gladwell takes a common subject, the story of people's successes, and uses an uncommon word to describe it.

Wherever possible, try to find words and themes that describe your subject matter in an uncommon way. This will add some flair to your title and cover.

> Find words and themes that describe your subject matter in an uncommon way.

3. Make a Statement—Use Emotion

The biggest sin in marketing is being *boring*. Do not be afraid to provoke a reaction in your cover and title. If your subject is controversial, then do not shy from the controversy. If you have convictions about your subject (and you do!), then make your statement.

Magnets attract, but magnets also repel. Do not be afraid to repel those who are not your ideal client and so attract your perfect audience.

4. Get Feedback

What a great time to be alive. It's easier than ever to attract a tribe and find communities that are likeminded. If that's true (and it is), then you should use that to your advantage at every turn.

I also recommend to my clients to use our private Facebook page and give several options to our seasoned authors to choose from. Try different title and cover options and ask your followers what they like and why. You will often be surprised at the results of your query.

5. Personal Preference but Use a Professional

What you desire and what looks good to you is always important. If you are in your field of expertise for any length of time, then you should have a good feel for what works and what doesn't. You want to create something that you really love and are going to be proud of promoting.

Your color selection is a key component of your book cover.

With that said, do not underestimate the importance of paying a professional graphic artist to do it right. There are low-cost alternatives for cover design, such as fiverr.com, and I would only use a low-cost provider if I already knew exactly what I wanted. You cannot expect great creativity on your project if you are paying only a few dollars.

A word about colors. Your color selection is a key component of your book cover. Here are some basics about colors. Remember rules are made to be broken, so use this as a loose guideline.

Red is a primary power color. It gets a person's attention and holds it. It is the most popular color for marketing and more red books are sold than other colors. That's just a fact.

Blue is a great color to be used to convey a feeling of trust and trustworthiness. It can be a great color if you are in coaching, counseling, or consulting.

If you're vying for the attention of a female demographic, you can't go wrong with **pink**. Obviously, it's a fun color and attractive to the eye. My client Kaelin Tuell of ladyboss.com uses it abundantly and with amazing results.

Orange is dynamic, positive, and optimistic.

Yellow is a power color, but you need to be really careful with yellow. You can make a lot of mistakes with that. We generally avoid yellow.

Green is fairly versatile. It's a warm and inviting color, conveying nature and health.

White is clean, simple, and straightforward. You see many of Gladwell's covers with white as the dominant color.

Maybe you've considered what colors you want. If you've already had a graphic artist design your cover, and you haven't considered what your color conveys, then I suggest you take another look.

Resources for Book Cover Designs

Let's look at a couple of options for you to have your cover designed. We'll also look at a couple of tips regarding those options.

99designs

The platform of 99designs is a great place to get graphic design work done. It's simple, as you can see when you visit: 99designs.com/book-cover-design.

You can browse designs that have already been created and get a feel for what you can expect. I have used this site for a number of designs of logos, websites, and books.

With 99designs, you set up a design contest, in which you give your parameters. Designers then create their version of what you want and submit it to you for review.

First, your feedback on the designs submitted is absolutely crucial. When you start getting designs from designers, they're going to ask you to rate the design and to give feedback.

The more feedback you give at the beginning, the better idea all the *other* designers will have, and they will begin designing based on your feedback.

The great thing about this process is, once you start giving the positive feedback, then all the designers jump in and they start using that feedback to give you exactly what you're looking for.

Second, you will want to guarantee your contest.

This might seem risky, but I've never had a problem with it and have found it brings in many of the best designers to compete for your business.

When you run a contest and you don't guarantee it, if you don't see anything you like, then you don't lose any money. You don't pick anybody, and nobody wins, however, the best designers often do not compete in these contests, and so the number of examples and quality is lower.

Once you guarantee the contest, there will be a flood of great designers who jump in, because they know somebody is going to win it.

While 99designs offers higher quality and more creative designs, you get to have your project competed for by dozens of different designers all working on your project.

fiverr.com

A lower-end option is fiverr.com.

Simply put, I would not suggest you use fiverr for your book cover, unless you are on a tight budget and know exactly what you want.

As said earlier, you can hardly expect anyone to spend much creative energy on your cover for $5–$10. There are some excellent designers on fiverr, and if you find one who has already created a cover that is similar to what you want, then it is worth a try.

Just remember that your book will be judged by its cover, so don't skimp here.

Obviously, if you have your own professional graphic designer (like BSP does), then that's the simplest way, because you can get exactly what you need, and you can send it back to your designer a hundred times, if need be. Thanks, Steve!

Launch Time

At this point, you have the title and the cover you want, your reviews are done, and your pricing strategy is all set. Time to set up all the traffic for your five-day promo launch.

The final three things we will be covering are all to be set and done for the five-day period of the KDP launch: press releases, free and paid advertising, and your social media strategy.

Press Releases

The press release service that we suggest and use is WebWire. There are others available, such as Cision PRWeb, but we have found that we get the best reach for the money with WebWire.

With Webwire, our press releases are syndicated to hundreds of media outlets and usually picked up by 100–150, each reaching tens of thousands of people. It is a wonderful way to get extra attention on your book launch.

This text is from WebWire's website.

> *Press Release distribution offered by WebWire primarily delivers your news to targeted media (reporters, registered media and trade publications) and media only wire services (accessed by leading print, broadcast and online publications) powered by our unique partnership with PR Newswire. Getting the media to respond to your message affords the highest degree of credibility.*

One thing of note. Press releases are sources of news, not marketing and advertising, and must be written in such a way. Let's discuss how to write your press releases so it has the greatest chance of being picked up by the media.

> Press releases are sources of news, not marketing and advertising, and must be written in such a way.

Three Press Releases Strategy

We recommend a strategy to use three press releases that works like this.

Our first press release is distributed on the day the promotion begins to announce the promotion opportunity.

Our second press release is distributed on day three of the promotion. This press release announces the book as a bestseller (this typically happens on the first day of the launch) and that the promotion is continuing for only two more days.

Then, our third press release is distributed on the last day of the promotion, stating that the promotion of this bestselling book is ending.

Each press release builds on the former release and creates urgency for the reader to take advantage of the promotion.

Writing Your Press Releases—First Release

Let's dive into how you write your press releases.

Your Press Release Title

First is, of course, your title.

Think of your press release title as your headline. The idea is that you want to hook those who are reading the press release with the information in your book title.

The first press release mentions the debut of your new book. We use the title of the book and explain that the book will be free to download tomorrow.

Be sure to give the date of the beginning of your promotion and put that in the title of the release, because some people will be reading your press release a day or two after it actually releases and launches.

I also recommend adding your name, along with the book title, in the first sentence of your press release. We do this for the online search engine optimization (SEO) benefits.

If possible, you want to hyperlink your press release title with the URL of your Amazon book. This way, someone can simply click through and go directly to Amazon to download your book.

By the way, one of the great benefits of doing press releases is that they will remain in the search engines for months and, in some cases, years!

When I search the title of one of my books or even my name, invariably I find press releases that we did two or three years ago that are still active and still highly optimized!

So, anytime someone clicks on that, even years from now, it will go directly to my Amazon page and they'll buy my book!

> One of the great benefits of doing press releases is that they will remain in the search engines for months and, in some cases, years!

Keywords in the Press Release

You're encouraged to hyperlink up to three words in your press release, so you will want to choose three keywords to link directly to your Amazon URL. This also helps with the SEO of your press release, and it also helps to better inform a media source that might be interested in picking up your press release.

Various media sources might be interested in the specific keywords for stories they are doing and might find your press release when searching for those keywords. Remember, you get excellent SEO and a good opportunity to rank for those keywords.

Discuss Details of the Book

In the body of the press release, list the newsworthy attributes of the book. Who the content helps, how the content will be helpful, and anything that makes a statement or provokes emotion.

Your Amazon book description is a good resource to use for the body of your press release.

List Two Book Reviews and Review Ratings

By now, your book has a minimum of 7–10 reviews with good ratings, so you will want to mention the average rating for your book reviews.

What we always do and recommend, for social proof, is to also list two or three of your best reviews right in your press release. Simply copy and paste the full reviews, typos and all, right into the press release.

Contact Information

In this section of the press release, you will want to add your business contact information. Be sure to add your name (or the person who will be handling all inquiries), business address, business phone number, and hyperlinked website URL.

About the Author

In this area, you want to tell the readers about yourself and give the readers reason to trust that you're the expert. You can, obviously, come up with something specific having to do with this particular book and why you wrote it, or you can just have a great general bio.

> Give the readers reason to trust that you're the expert.

Second and Third Press Releases

The second and third press releases are going to be similar to the first release, and I will only be discussing the elements that should be changed.

Title of Press Release

You're going to change the title in the second and third press releases, because (if we did everything right) the book is now an Amazon bestseller, and you want to announce that in the title.

You can also add (if it's the last day of the promo) that it's free for one more day. Or if there are a couple of days left, because it's day three of the promo, you can say that "This bestselling book is available for two more days."

Either way, you want to change the title to reflect this.

New Reviews

The second thing you want to change is the book reviews that you had in the first press release.

With each press release, you're going to list two or three new reviews that are going to change the press release enough to give it some new wording, which will help with SEO and result in additional media outlets picking up the press release.

So, really, only a few things need to change within your press releases. If you do the first press release right and include all the hyperlinks, then you'll see some really great results.

Title: Announce that your book will be free tomorrow. Give a date just incase theyare reading it a day or 2 later.	Red Flags, Will Be Free to Download Tomorrow (11/03/2014)

Red Flags, Will Be Free to Download Tomorrow (11/03/2014)

[Like 0] [Tweet 1]   [g+1 0]   [Share 0] [Submit]

I like to have the Authors name as well as the book's title in the first sentence of the PR. Remember to hyperlink the title with the URL to your Amazon book. Good for SEO.

United States – WEBWIRE – Sunday, November 02, 2014

Richard Mabbun and Julian Makas is proud to present their newest book, "Red Flags, Recognize and eliminate the risks in your RIA firm's Disaster Recovery, IT Compliance, and Cyber Security processes to safeguard your reputation and client trust."

Richard and Julian wrote Red Flags for the owners and officers of any Registered Investment Advisory firm; this book seeks to provide the answers you need to safeguard your firm's reputation and maintain your clients' trust.

Keywords:
Pick out 3 keywords to hyperlink to your Amazon URL. Helps with SEO as well as who picks up your Press Release.

With over 35 combined years of reviewing and protecting RIA firms, Richard and Julian understands the unique cyber security threats, compliance regulations, and resource constraints facing RIA firms, which compelled them to share their knowledge.

Their hope is that by reading this book, you'll become better educated on the technology risks threatening your firm so you can proactively take action to protect your firm's valuable internal and client related data, meet all regulatory compliance standards, and sleep better at night.

Important Paragraph:
Announce the specifics of your promotion. Give the date, Hyperlink the book URL, and book's rating.

Richard and Julian Makas' "Red Flags" will be free and available for download on Amazon for 5 days (11/03/2014 – 11/07/2014) at: http://www.amazon.com/dp/B00NMW28WG Red Flags is rated a 4.9 by those who have purchased the book. Here's what some of the reviewers have said:

Reviews:
This is your social proof. Show 2 to 3 reviews that have been left for you on your Amazon page.

"A wonderful and practical guide to information security and systems management. I learned a lot and appreciated the level at which the insights were delivered. It was not at all too technical. It was fast paced and an easy read. The red flags concept is a brilliant one - know what to look out for, and what questions to ask based on the many 'red flags' Richard and Julian have been exposed to through their work with businesses on matters related to security and systems management. I have to go now. Off to change all my passwords. Thank you for that wake up call I needed that." – Adam Mosley

"RIA which stands for (Rich Internet Application) is a must have program for backups, disaster recovery and cyber security. With all the computer hacking these days with big corporations, you can never be too safe. This book is for ideal for those who are computer savvy and administrators. Excellent read." – B. Camp

Contact Information:
Give your contact information.

For More Information: For more questions or to schedule an interview about this press release please contact Rebecca, Author Liaison, at (626) 765-9750 or email info@bestsellerpublishing.org

About the Author:
Tell the readers about yourself. Take this time to convince your readers to trust that you are the expert and that your content will help them.

About The Author: Richard Mabbun is CEO and co-founder of ITEGRIA, a firm which offers technology and security support services exclusively to RIA firms. He has over two decades of experience in deploying technology to address compliance issues affecting the financial services market in general and independent investment advisors specifically. Richard is a frequent invited speaker on the subject of technology efficiencies, challenges, and risks to RIA offices.

Julian Makas is COO and co-founder of ITEGRIA. He is an enthusiastic leader and manager who has worked the entire spectrum of information technology helping corporations and SMBs attain their goals of implementing secure technologies and systems. With over 18 years of in-depth information systems exposure, Julian frequently speaks on topics such as cyber-security and his firsthand experience on how drastically the evolution of technology has affected the world around us.

Press Release

WebWire

Let's take a minute and talk about the potential reach of a press release with WebWire.

In a recent press release that BSP did for a client, less than a week ago, we got 68,716 headline impressions and 2,036 reads—all in less than one week.

This press release is still active and, the great thing is, you can see all the different agencies that have picked up and run this press release. This means that people who've gone to their website have also read this exact press release.

It also means that you can mention on your website (for credibility and positioning purposes) that you were featured in any of these websites.

For example, this press release was featured in the *Miami Herald* and *Investor's Business Daily*. Often, radio and television (depending on the topic) will also pick up the press release.

There are typically well over 100 of these that will be featuring you and your book from just one WebWire press release, which you can then use as social proof on your website or book site. Press releases are a great strategy and quite powerful for many reasons.

Free and Paid Advertising

Our next step for our traffic campaign during our five-day KDP promotion is free and paid advertising.

I often teach on webinars and trainings that the difference between traditional publishing and BSP is (among other things) traditional publishers expect you to already have a large platform before they publish your book. In contrast, what we teach at BSP is how to actually use your book to grow a large platform.

> What we teach at BSP is how to actually use your book to grow a large platform.

Let me give you an example. Let's say that you decided to write a book on your expertise: corporate culture. You want to market it but, unfortunately, have a small following and client list.

A quick online search on the topic of top corporate culture blogs gives 18,800,000 results. Well, we don't need that many, so let's try the first one that lists the top 20 corporate culture blogs. By the way, I pulled this example out of the air and literally did it as I wrote this section of the book.

Back to our example. If we looked at the top 20 corporate culture blogs, we find that the first one is tinypulse.com, a website I have never heard of. A quick search on similarweb.com, and I find that tinypulse.com gets over 630,000 visitors every single month. Not only that but it has 35,000 Twitter followers and 4,800 Facebook followers.

So, what are we doing in this example? We are seeing that no matter what topic or expertise you decide to write on, there are blogs, websites, and podcasts, where people have already been creating content and writing about these subjects for years. They have already grown a following and now are looking to monetize it. All you have to do is put your content in front of them.

If you were to place a small, relatively inexpensive ad for a short period of time in front of these people who have already raised their hands and said, "I am interested in this specific topic of conversation," then you will get results.

When you've optimized your cover and title to attract your ideal customer, and then you put that cover and title and your ad in front of that customer, then invariably you're going to have people who leave that platform to buy your book.

You can use your book to build your platform.

Now, to be honest, I have started with the more advanced strategy. It is one I highly recommend but not for your KDP launch. I would recommend the previous strategy in conjunction with a free-plus-shipping funnel or a funnel to drive customers to a free consultative call. You see, the absolute best potential customers will be on a blog or website like the one we just searched.

You can use your book to build your platform.

In fact, there are several strategies you can use to attract these potential customers, including becoming a regular contributor to the blog (similar to the strategy discussed at the beginning of this chapter in Bill Stack's story) or even simply to be interviewed as an expert, something I will discuss in greater detail in the Profit phase.

With all that said, how would you like a shortcut?

Thought so. The best way to launch your KDP promotion is to other authors and book buyers who have raised their hands and requested to be informed whenever a new promotion is run. There are literally millions of people who have signed up to be notified when new books on various topics are on a KDP promotion.

Here are a few of the *paid* options.

- BookBub—tough acceptance criteria but large and legitimate list—better for .99 promotion rather than the KDP
- ManyBooks—application required but large email list and over 400,000 views per month
- BookGoodies—simple process and nice following
- Books Butterfly—millions of readers and prorated based on response
- Freebooksy—large following, multiple genres

Here are a few of the *free* options.

- Indie Author News—solid following and multiple genres
- Digital Book Today—requires 20 four-plus star reviews
- EbooksHabit—five reviews required
- The eReader Cafe—requires three reviews with 3.5+ average
- Ebook Korner Kafé—large Facebook and social media following

These are just a few of the literally hundreds of options that a simple online search will uncover.

Social Media Strategy

Let's talk about social media.

First, much of what was discussed in the above section applies to social media. Massive followings have been built on Facebook, Twitter, Instagram, and LinkedIn that can be a perfect source for your book and personal promotions.

Let's hit some basics.

First, you should have a Facebook page, a Twitter account, and other social media presence for your book and your business. This is separate and distinct from your personal pages. Though there is nothing wrong with also promoting your book on your personal pages.

A quick search on Facebook (or any social media platform) for Kindle, book promotion, or book marketing groups will turn up dozens of groups that you should join. BSP owns several of these groups that have almost 100,000 members. The biggest mistake I see is authors' laziness resulting in them spamming these pages and groups and getting absolutely zero results. They are called social sites for a reason. You must be social and build relationships. If you do that with other likeminded individuals, then you will have the opportunity to reach their networks during your promotion periods. Resist the desire to spam and instead build alliances.

Follow the same pattern and process as discussed in the previous section and you will find both paid and free opportunities to promote your book during the book promotion phase.

There is work for you to do in this phase. Find the right websites, blogs, and social media to market to in the five-day promo period. If you wish to have a virtuous cycle, then start it off right and do the work. The rewards are amazing!

Section Three

Profit

CHAPTER 8

Fiesta (Birthday) Time

"Money has never been an issue with me.
I will make and continue to make plenty
of money."

—MC Hammer

My wife, Connie, and I have three boys, ages 26, 23, and 17. My absolute favorite tradition is how we celebrate one another's birthdays. You might guess (correctly) that my birthday is my favorite, but all of them are special.

Each year, we have a family-only dinner (besides whatever group occasions we choose to do), and during dinner we each take a few moments and share a special characteristic or trait about the birthday person that makes them special to us.

This past year, as we celebrated Jake's birthday (he's the 23-year-old), it was more of the usual fun and shenanigans. We each shared about Jake's work ethic (he is in his final year of college at the University of California, San Diego (UCSD), majoring in math and physics, while also working remotely for NASA and the Jet Propulsion Laboratory (JPL); yes *that* NASA), his kindness, and other attributes we appreciated about him.

It came time to have dessert and the waitstaff brought over a cake with a single candle in it. We asked Jake to make a wish and blow out the candle, so we could eat some dessert. Jake took a deep breath and started to blow, and then abruptly stopped. He seemed to think to himself for a moment and then took another deep breath to blow, and then stopped again. Now anything that gets in the way of me eating dessert tends to annoy me, so I asked him, "Jake, what's up?"

He said, "You know, it's weird. Just when I was about to wish for something, I thought, I don't need to wish for that, I just need to get out there and go to work for that and I'll have it!"

I looked at Connie, and I gave her this huge high-five at the table and said, "Yes, that's what I'm talking about. Maybe we did something right after all! Oh, and get me some dessert!"

By the way, I highly recommend you adding this tradition to your family. If you have boys, like me, it might be the only time you ever get to hear what you might have done right!

The simple lesson in this (true) story must be applied to your book and whatever you hope to accomplish with your book.

Too many authors think their book is a magic bean that once done and planted will automatically and without effort produce everything they ever wanted. And while no one would ever declare such a thing, I tell you that most authors' actions (or lack thereof) declare it.

Your book is the greatest tool you will ever have to produce results for you and

> Your book is the greatest tool you will ever have to produce results for you and your business to accomplish your dreams and goals even beyond your imagination.

your business to accomplish your dreams and goals even beyond your imagination. So, we must do something with it!

What do we do then? I'm glad you asked.

We focus on three primary things in the profit phase.

1. Speaking engagements
2. Free publicity
3. Lead generation

From these three actions, we have myriad opportunities and directions we can go. The remainder of the book will be dedicated to showing you how and giving you examples to follow.

Before we dive into them, we need to clarify some ideas.

Once your book is launched and becomes a bestseller, it is no longer about the book. Let me repeat that. Once your book is launched and hits bestseller, then we no longer focus on the book.

The book is a great dichotomy. On the one hand, it is your greatest source of credibility and authority. Yet, on the other hand, it is the cheapest way someone can enter your world.

Authors often ask me after the book launch how they can keep their book selling. And there are actually many ways to do so. For example, if you have a speaking engagement, then you can pitch your book and sell it. But I always ask, "Why would you do that?"

You see, if you sell a high-value, high-priced consulting program, then your best interest is to use the book to generate leads that might get you checks of $10,000, $20,000, or even $100,000. Do you have any idea how many books you'd have to sell to earn that?

Once the book is done and launched to bestseller, it is no longer about the book.

Now it is about *you*!

1. Shelf Life vs. No Shelf Life

The attention your book gets (and, consequently, your book's status as a bestseller) has a lifespan.

If you were to check right now as to whether the first Harry Potter book is on the bestseller list, you'd find that it's not. It sold over 100 million copies, but it too, even with that many copies sold, has a shelf life.

Your book, and the attention and focus it gets, is going to have a lifespan, but here's the cool thing: *your status as a bestselling author does not.*

And that status as a bestselling author can be used to get exactly what you're looking for in terms of speaking engagements, free publicity, and lead generation for your products, your services, your consulting, and your business for as long as you wish.

2. Set Objectives

Once you understand what the focus is, you are free to set true objectives for your business and use of the book.

So, what is it that you really want? What do you want your life and business to look like in one year, three years, and five years? Do you want to be a speaker? Have you thought through what that might mean travelwise? How do you generate leads for your business right now? How can you incorporate the book into those systems or, better yet, build entirely new systems around the book?

You need some specific targets to aim at, so that you can get exactly what you want from your bestselling book on a continual basis.

3. Build Systems

Without question, you are going to get a bump in business and opportunities from your book launch. Ted Kallman and Andrew Kallman got multiple speaking engagements and new clients totaling over $250,000 in revenue. Not bad, yet they didn't write a book for just a one-time bump.

You need systems that give you consistency in activity, which give you consistency in your results.

I talk to so many business owners that are up and down in their incomes. They have a big month and they have a down month, big month, down month.

You see that a lot in businesses because they're inconsistent in their activities, whether it be marketing, PR, or sales activities. You must think in terms of implementing some simple systems on a regular basis, so that you don't have inconsistent results and do things reactively.

MC Hammer thought he would always make money because of his momentary fame. Let's be proactive with our focus and build something for the long haul.

CHAPTER 9

Options, Options, and More Options

> "The only thing worse than being blind is having sight but no vision."
>
> —Helen Keller

While I'm going to go into detail in the next few chapters on speaking engagements, media, and generating leads in a variety of ways, I wanted to make sure that you see just how many options you really have to generate income with your book.

It seems that almost every client of mine is doing it in a slightly different way, usually based on their strengths and the assets in their businesses.

Here are a few of their examples.

Royalties

I always tell my clients to expect little to nothing when it comes to earning royalties on their books. Perhaps that's an innate desire to underpromise and overdeliver. Truth be told, I have sold about 40,000 copies of my first book and continue to get royalties every month put into my bank account by our friends at Amazon. My largest monthly royalty check was over $1,000. Not bad for doing something one time, over ten years ago. Thanks, Amazon.

Self-published authors are actually outearning all the major traditional publishing houses combined. As I said earlier, Amazon sells over 1,000,000 ebooks (not including softcover and hardcover) every single day.

There is a reason it is the largest company in the world.

Just remember, I said you probably won't make much in royalties, so go out and do something proactively.

Paid Speaking Engagements

My business partner and friend, Kevin Harrington of *Shark Tank* fame was completely behind the scenes prior to writing his first book. Kevin was the original shark on the hit TV show *Shark Tank*. The inventor of the infomercial, and the iconic figure behind such amazing infomercials as the Ginsu knives, the George Foreman grill, and Tony Little fitness products, having sold over five billion dollars of products.

What many people don't realize is that Kevin, though he had sold five billion dollars' worth of products, was completely unknown, because he was always the guy behind the camera. In 2009, he published his first book, *Act Now! How I Turn Ideas into Million-Dollar Products*, and that book landed on the desk of executive producer Mark Burnett of *Survivor*. It was the tipping point that got Kevin his gig on *Shark Tank*, and, to this day, now almost 10 years later, has positioned him as a top-five business speaker in the country, earning fees of up to $50,000 per speech, and speaking 50 to 75 times a year all over the country. Do the math on that!

Kevin had desired to finally move from behind the camera to in front of the camera. And his first bestselling book in 2009 is what did it for him.

Free Speaking Engagements

Speaking for free is actually my preferred way of making money with speaking. I know that might seem a little confusing, but there are a number of ways to make big money speaking. Being paid to speak is actually the hardest.

> Selling from a stage enables you to earn as much as you want, based on your level of skill speaking from the stage.

Selling from a stage enables you to earn as much as you want, based on your level of skill speaking from the stage. My friend, mentor, and client Russell Brunson (cofounder of ClickFunnels) recently spoke on sales trainer Grant Cardone's stage at the 10X Growth Conference in Las Vegas. He sold $3.5 million in 90 minutes from the stage. If you can sell from the stage, then you can get as many speaking engagements as are worth your while.

My client Mike Dieterich is not trained to sell from the stage, but he did it a completely different way.

Mike is an environmental scientist and owns Renew and Sustain, an environmental consulting company. Mike consults with governments, municipalities, school districts, and builders on how they can reduce their carbon footprint and become a more energy friendly construction project.

Mike wanted to speak at the Green Festival, which routinely has an attendance of 20,000 to 30,000 people and features the biggest names in his industry. Mike's desire was to speak on stage, so he could get in front of his ideal clients, which are C-suite executives of these firms.

Mike came to us to get his first book done, appropriately titled, *Renew and Sustain: A Cutting Edge Approach to Being Socially Responsible, Environmentally Conscious, and Incredibly Profitable for Businesses, Schools and Government,* which we launched to international bestseller a couple of years ago. At the same time, our PR department booked Mike on several TV spots, radio, and industry-related blogs. With the bestselling book and publicity, we were able to help Mike get featured as a keynote speaker at the Green Festival in Washington, DC, with an attendance of over 20,000 people.

Mike spoke at that event, and then was asked to be the keynote speaker for the Green Festivals in Portland, Oregon; Los Angeles, California; and San Francisco, and in that year spoke to over 100,000 people. Mike's opportunities to grow his business actually didn't come from the people who were at the event, but they came from the sponsors of the event. You see, the sponsors were his ideal clients. They were the builders, the municipalities, and the construction companies that needed Mike's services. As an author and the featured keynote speaker, they saw Mike as the authority in the space and reached out to him for his services. His business exploded.

Consulting

A large percentage of our clients are coaches and consultants in numerous industries. Consultants need to have authority in their space, because many times they are working with successful

Nothing is better than a book to create that authority and credibility.

people who run large companies. Nothing is better than a book to create that authority and credibility.

Joel and Julie Landi are successful corporate culture and relationship consultants in Los Angeles, California. When they decided to start their consulting business, though experienced, they needed a book to use as a tool to drive leads and opportunities for the growth of the business. Joel authored *Rewired: Power Up Your Performance, Relationships, and Purpose.*

The plan was to work with C-suite executives from mid-sized corporations (up to $100M per year) and simply introduce themselves by sending the executives their book. In the first year of using the book in this way, they did over $300,000 in revenue.

Joel also gets paid and free speaking engagements using his book. He only speaks to his ideal audience, so it can lead to conversations and opportunities for more consulting agreements.

Coaching

While similar to consulting, coaching offers an opportunity to help all kinds of people based on your area of success and expertise. My dear friend and client Shanda Sumpter uses the book we helped her create, *Core Calling: Your Step by Step Plan to Building a Business That Sets You Up for Life!,* to generate leads for her highly successful coaching business.

Shanda does most of her marketing online and in her own live event. Online Shanda offers a digital version of her bestselling book for free or individuals can order a softcover version of the book for free, as long as they pay shipping costs.

Afterwards, those that requested a copy of Shanda's book are followed up with by her sales team and given a free coaching call. After the call, if they are a fit for her program, they are offered a chance to join her coaching program for an investment of $10,000.

In the first four months of using her book and this process, she generated over 11,000 leads and sold over $400,000 in coaching services. Sweet! I give more details of Shanda's funnel in a later chapter.

Your Own Live Events

Live events that you run to meet and address your ideal client continue to be one of the best ways to attract clients and grow a business. In fact, this year at BSP we will have 12 live events and, by doing so, will add an additional $1,000,000 (or more) to our bottom line.

My client Pedro Adao, a financial planner, does something similar. Pedro is the bestselling author of *The Finished Life: An Adventure into Identity, Purpose, and Power.* It's not unusual for financial planners to do small, live events and often will host them at upscale restaurants to attract potential clients.

Pedro had been doing this in the past but stopped because he found it getting increasingly expensive and difficult to fill the room and it stopped being profitable.

Pedro made some changes and began advertising and giving away his bestselling book at the event. He saw an immediate spike in both attendance and the quality of his attendees. The book featured him as a bestseller and expert on his topic and attracted more of the right people to his audience. He used this process throughout 2017 and ended up doing over a million dollars in income from this simple change.

Raising Money

I shared earlier about Doug Bowman and John Mullen and their book, *Florencia: An Accidental Story*. In the first six months, they raised over $250,000 for their brand-new charity, got connected to the president of Mozambique, and will address the General Assembly of the United Nations in the next month. All this was accomplished by using their bestselling book to open the right doors.

My client Amir Baluch does it for a different reason. Amir is an anesthesiologist and avid real estate investor. He and many of his doctor friends have invested in real estate together and done well.

Amir wanted to grow this into a business, helping doctors secure their retirement with real estate, but could never seem to raise money outside of his direct sphere of influence. So, we helped him launch his bestselling book, *Make It, Keep It: The New Rules of Wealth Preservation for Doctors*.

Amir began mailing his book to groups and associations (and individuals) of doctors and setting appointments to discuss what he does. Within the first six months of using the book, Amir raised over $2,000,000 for real estate investing. In fact, he was recently in LA to visit and purchase some real estate for the group in Beverly Hills.

Building Your Audience

A big focus this year for BSP and me is to create valuable content for my audience. The book, of course, but also a daily podcast, video show, and blog. This is perhaps the best and easiest time to quickly and profitably grow your own audience.

We helped my client Lou Diamond write and market his bestselling book, *Master the Art of Connecting* in 2016. About the same time, Lou decided to start a podcast and used the book and authority from it to attract high-level guests to his show.

In less than a year, Lou's podcast, Thrive LOUD, has become a top-five business podcast on iTunes and routinely connects him with high-level guests. On a recent phone call, Lou shared that he just signed a $50,000 consulting agreement because of the book and podcast and has been asked to be a paid speaker a number of times from listeners of the podcast. Time to start building your own platform perhaps.

Connect with Thought Leaders and Joint Venture Partners

Perhaps the fastest way to grow your business is to connect with people who already serve the same clients that you do, but in a different capacity, and joint venture or partner together.

Kevin Harrington of *Shark Tank* and I did that together about eight months ago. We reached out to each other to see if there was a way to help some of his clients who were interested in writing a book and getting an endorsement from him.

> Perhaps the fastest way to grow your business is to connect with people who already serve the same clients that you do.

We came up with the idea to partner on an anthology series of books, where Kevin would write a chapter and be the face and celebrity of the book and also offer a video endorsement of the author. This offered the authors the authority of being connected with Kevin Harrington and a contributor in his latest bestselling book. In the first eight months of this partnership, we have done over $250,000 in revenue.

My client John Rizvi, a patent attorney and author of *Think and Grow Rich for Inventors*, reached out to me to see if there might also be a way to work with Kevin, because Kevin is an icon in John's field.

We brought John into the latest anthology book and got him an endorsement video from Kevin. That video has already been viewed over 20,000 times by John's potential clients. John has been able to grow his lead generation and sales massively from that book and video endorsement.

These are just a few of the many interesting ways our clients are using their books to make money, connect with thought leaders, and grow their platforms.

Over the next few chapters, we will discuss in detail how to get speaking engagements, generate free publicity, attract leads to your business, and so grow your income and make an impact in this world.

CHAPTER 10

The Power of Speaking

"The secret of being boring
is to say everything."

—**Voltaire**

There is something to standing on stage, above the crowd and lifted up as a bestselling author and expert on a topic. It is powerful positioning and irresistible to your ideal clients. Furthermore, what many people do not realize is that having a book is often a prerequisite to even having the potential to get on a stage in the first place—this is true for TED and TEDx Talks and many large conferences and trade shows.

It can be a rush too.

More than that though, it is perhaps your greatest opportunity to connect with high-level influencers and clients, especially if what you sell is an expensive service, product, or consulting.

Richard Mabbun is the CEO and founding partner of ĪTEGRIA, which provides management and expertise to small and mid-sized investment advisory firms. He is also the bestselling author of *Red Flags: Recognize and Eliminate the Risks in Your RIA Firm's Disaster Recovery, IT Compliance, and Cyber Security Processes to Safeguard Your Reputation and Client Trust.*

Richard's firm primarily helps mid-size financial advisory firms with cybersecurity and platform management. An average client invests $50,000 per year with his company, for these valuable services.

Richard's goal in coming to us was to create a bestselling book that gave him the credibility to be asked to speak at industry events and trade shows, where his ideal client was going to learn the latest techniques and procedures for cybersecurity.

After the publishing and launch of Richard's book, he was able to start speaking on his preferred stages and immediately saw massive results. Here is what he had to say.

> *You and your team promised to have everything done and true to your word the book launched on time and on the exact day that I needed it to launch. In less than one day, the book became an Amazon bestseller. Being a bestselling author and offering a book gave us immediate credibility to our prospects, and my company was able to leverage that to raise a large number of leads from our speaking engagements. We were able to close more than 14 clients from one particular trade show, and since each client has an average yearly value of more than $50,000 to our firm, that made an immediate impact on our business.*

I'd say! That's $700,000 in yearly income from one speaking event.

The Importance of Choosing the Right Opportunity

I've had the unique opportunity to be a guest speaker and host a roundtable for Russell Brunson's flagship event, Funnel Hacking Live. In 2018, Funnel Hacking Live had over 3,000 participants. Each time I've hosted that roundtable event, I've met droves of potential clients and done over $100,000 in business for BSP.

I don't speak often, because I don't like to travel for business, so most of what I do is our live events locally in Pasadena. In 2017, I had the opportunity to do a local speaking engagement for 60 minutes and be paid $5,000 to address a company's national sales representatives in Orange County, California. Of course, to earn $5,000 in just 60 minutes and do it locally was appealing to me, so I accepted.

Unfortunately, I didn't check my schedule (because who does that?), so I booked the event, signed the contract, and was sent the $5,000 check long before the event ever took place. Little did I realize that I was already booked for that exact day. I mean, come on, I speak so infrequently, what are the odds?

When I finally did check my schedule, I found that the 2017 Funnel Hacking Live event was going to be held at the same time as the national sales event that I was supposed to speak at in Orange County for the $5,000 fee.

Many authors come to me and tell me that what they desire more than anything else is to be paid to speak. OK, fine. Yet, consider for a moment the lifestyle that is required to make just a few hundred thousand dollars per year.

For example, if you're going to be paid $5,000–$10,000 per speech, to earn $300,000 you will need to be on the road 30 weeks a year. I don't know about you, but that's something, quite frankly, I'm not interested in doing. In my opinion, it's hardly worth it, and there are better and easier ways to earn the same money.

You have to really consider what your best opportunities are when it comes to speaking and where you can get the biggest bang for your buck. I lived up to my contract and I spoke at that local sales conference and earned my $5,000, but I missed the day that I was supposed to be presenting at Funnel Hacking Live.

Though I was not paid a guaranteed sum for Funnel Hacking Live, I most certainly missed an opportunity to earn much more than the $5,000 I was paid at that event. Even though the money isn't guaranteed, when you are speaking in front of your ideal audience and you have a compelling offer, you can make far more money speaking for free than you ever can speaking for a fee.

Simple System for Speaking Engagements

Now, you will have to choose for yourself which you want, but, as my example above, make sure you choose wisely. With that said, either way we need some kind of system set up so we can get these opportunities on a regular basis and not haphazardly. The more opportunities you get, the choosier you can be.

> The more opportunities you get, the choosier you can be.

Let's spend a few minutes discussing a simple system that, if you do it consistently, will produce as many speaking engagements as you could ever want.

There are three core components of our speaking system.

1. Target
2. Assets
3. Process

Let's discuss each one in detail.

T.A.P. SYSTEM

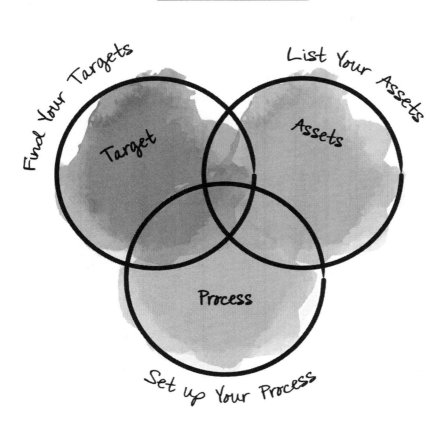

Target Assets Process

Target

The first step in the process is to determine where exactly it is best for you to speak. There are approximately 30,000 conferences and trade shows that take place in the US every single year. There is a plethora of opportunity for you, but only if you know what they are and what you want.

We suggest coming up with three tiers of targets.

Tier one (bullseye) is any direct public or private organization that is your ideal client who is holding an event or has its own internal conferences or trainings. If you are a corporate coach or trainer, then this would be a corporation that is ideally suited for your specific and unique abilities.

Tier two (first outer ring) is any conference, trade show, or association that holds events that has your ideal client in the room to learn. If you trained Realtors, then this would be the National Association of Realtors (NAR) event or any number of local or regional events that the NAR puts on.

Tier three (second outer ring) is any local conference or event that has a mix of people who might be your potential client, but it is far less targeted. An example of this event would be a local chamber of commerce, or a Rotary or Lions Club event that has local businessowners but is not targeted to one specific kind of business. If you serve local businesses with your expertise, then this might be exactly what you are looking for.

Once you've determined your tier one, two, and three targets, then the next step is for you (or an assistant) to find the contact information for the decisionmaker of these events. You will need a name, address, telephone number, and email address. We suggest that you make a list of 100 of these event organizers and coordinators.

TIER 1,2,3

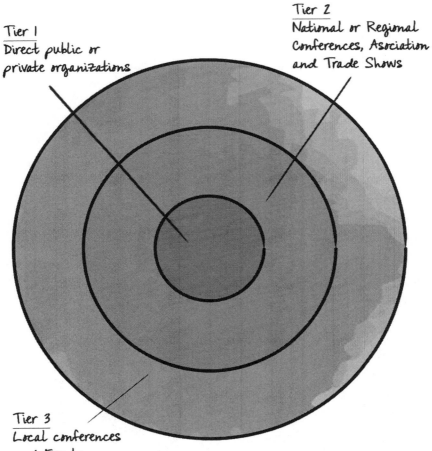

Tier 1
Direct public or
private organizations

Tier 2
National or Regional
Conferences, Association
and Trade Shows

Tier 3
Local conferences
and Events

Tier 1,2,3 Image

Assets

Next, we want to take account of our assets to make these contacts easier, if possible. Your assets are your past and present personal relationships.

For example, right now I am working on releasing a new licensed book program for people in the real estate profession, and my first step was to consider my relationship assets. Though I am not looking for speaking engagements per se, this exercise still applies. I've done a number of books for highly successful real estate coaches and broker owners, and so I simply started reaching out to my list. Within one week I was connected to the program director for the California Association of Realtors and set up a speaking engagement to launch the program to a large Realtor-only event. This all came directly from my own personal database without any cold contact.

Think of your assets in terms of the following.

- Current clients

- Past clients

- Email and mailing list

- Friends

- Family

- Sphere of influence

- Networking groups

- Social media following

Your goal will be find people within your relationships that are already directly in contact with or one-degree separated from your ideal clients.

So, start taking stock of what ways (and who can help) you can connect personally with your ideal places to speak. I am going to show you how to cold connect with them in a moment, but nothing is better than a warm introduction.

> Your goal will be find people within your relationships that are already directly in contact with or one-degree separated from your ideal clients.

Process

Once this work is done, and you have a list of 100 best opportunities and also what assets might directly connect you to those opportunities, it's time to set up a repeatable process or system that you can use to connect with them directly.

For our purposes, a process is a simple, repeatable, and consistent system that gets you a predictable result.

Here's the process.

Step one: Every week, you are going to mail a copy of your book directly to the decisionmaker of the event or conference. You are going to include a beautiful cover letter, and you are going to personalize the book with a sticky note on the front cover mentioning the individual by name and directing him or her to something valuable in the book.

Sticky note example: *"Hi, Jane, Thanks for taking a minute to look at this. Thought this might be helpful in light of your upcoming conference on sustainability. I address several of those specific topics on page 126. Let me know your thoughts. Talk soon, Mike."*

Now, what have we done here? Well, first and foremost, we have provided value to an influencer in our space without asking for anything. The law of reciprocity kicks in here, and this previously unknown person has received something of value from us that addresses a need he or she has.

Second, we have indirectly shown this person that we too are an influencer in this space (though he or she doesn't know us), because we have written a bestselling book on the topic. Something that more than likely he or she has not done.

You will send three to five books with these sticky notes every single week to different influencers. By the way, you can print a beautiful softcover edition of your book for about $3–$4 and send it for about $3 using USPS. At most this will cost you $50 per week, and you will be connecting with the most influential people in your space, every single week.

Step two: Two to three days after the book arrives, you will have your assistant follow up with a call to confirm that the book arrived and was received. If you do not have an assistant, then pay a virtual assistant for the one to two hours per week that this will require. It is far better for you to have your assistant speak to their assistant to set up a possible meeting or discussion.

Assistant script example: *Hi, may I speak to Ms. Jones? Oh, Ms. Jones is not available right now, I understand* (typically your assistant will be speaking to the gatekeeper, his or her assistant), *no problem. I simply wanted to make sure that Mike's book arrived and was received by Ms. Jones. Did she get it and have a chance to look at it? OK, great. Well, I thought it might be best to see if we can get Mike and Ms. Jones together for a quick chat to discuss your upcoming event. Fantastic. Which is better— 9 a.m. or 11 a.m. tomorrow?*

The goal here is for the book to facilitate a conversation in which you are viewed as an expert and valuable resource, rather than a nobody hoping to land a speaking engagement.

If you do this systematically, you will find that by the third or fourth week you will start booking engagements and perhaps even circumvent the process and start booking clients.

Resource

AssociationExecs.com allows you to do research about specific associations, so that you can target those associations and organizers directly.

And, within those associations are thousands and even tens of thousands of members who might be your ideal clients. There are some big opportunities with associations. You can also use this for your conference searches. See associationexecs.com/Meeting-Planners

From the site: *"Access not only the most up-to-date records on meeting planners, but also over 125,000 Association Executives, over 20,000 Associations and over 450 Association Management Firms!"*

How to Close When You Can't Close

Now, it's important to note that many conferences and association will not allow you to directly sell from the stage. However, this is not a problem when you are speaking in front of your ideal client. What we suggest to our clients is to create something that we call a client success pack.

For example, let's say that you're like our client, Richard Mabbun, speaking in front of a trade show, which will not allow him to directly pitch his services. Richard would leave 5–10 minutes at the end of his speech and use the following close.

At this point, I've given you the best information I can in the time allotted. Of course, both you and I know that there's much more that can be said about the topic of cybersecurity for your firm.

So, here's what I've done, with permission from the trade show organizers. I've created a cybersecurity success pack, and in the success pack I have included three things for you. Number one, I want to give you completely free, a copy of my bestselling book, Red Flags. Number two, I'd like to give you my free CD on the "Five Biggest Mistakes that RIA Firms Make That Put Their Client's Information at Risk." And number three, and probably the most valuable, is I want to give you 15 to 20 minutes of my time to discuss what your needs are and what questions you might directly have for your cybersecurity firm.

Right now, my assistants are passing out forms for you to get the cybersecurity success pack. Please take a moment, fill the form out, and hand it in at the back table. I don't have enough books with me to accommodate everyone, so include your mailing address. I will be mailing a copy of the full success pack to you within the next few days. Thanks for your time and attention.

Now, what we've done here is actually created something of great interest to our potential ideal clients in the audience by giving them something of great value. We are not simply handing out books to anyone. The only people who we are going to give this to are people who complete our form requesting the information.

Now, what should be on the form? Well, besides the name, telephone number, and mailing address, you will want to ask two or three questions on this form that allow you to determine the quality of this lead.

For example, Richard would want to know how large the RIA firm is, how many financial advisors are part of the firm, and perhaps he would also like to know the assets under management of the firm. He would do all this to determine exactly how good an ideal candidate this is for him. We've had clients close up to 85 percent of the room using the success pack offer that I've just shared with you.

Yes, it will cost a little money and you won't be selling books at the back of the table, but if your average client value is high, then this is the best use of your book.

> What we've done is actually created something of great interest to our potential ideal clients in the audience by giving them something of great value.

You now have a number of highly qualified leads that you will begin getting back in touch with, and, of course, after they filled out the form, the people who are the most qualified are those you're going to get back to the quickest.

Worth Noting . . .

My good friend and client Roddy Chong, author of the forthcoming book *Ovation: Unlocking the Hidden Secrets to Influencing the Masses*, is the lead violinist for Shania Twain, Celine Dion, and the Trans-Siberian Orchestra. Roddy is a professional speaker when he is not on tour (his presentation is one of the best I have ever heard and seen), and up until now Roddy has booked all his speaking engagements by cold calling conferences and organizations.

Roddy's speaking fees range up to $25,000, and he consistently gets booked because he is on the phone hustling. As soon as Roddy's book comes out, he will be implementing my system, but, in the meantime, he continues successfully cold calling.

My point is these opportunities are there for you for the taking. If you implement this system, it might be one of the most powerful things you ever do.

CHAPTER 11

Media Fame, Shall We?

"Fame itself . . . doesn't really afford
you anything more than a good seat
in a restaurant."

—David Bowie

A few years ago, Karen Simpson-Hankins came to us with a desire to grow her business and build her personal brand and profile. Karen is a 30-year veteran of the real estate and mortgage industry, and her desire was to grow substantially. We helped her launch her book, *Conquer Your Closing: Insider Secrets for Today's Savvy Home Buyer*, and it went exceptionally well. Karen became a number-one bestseller in real estate and five other categories.

During the launch, the conference organizer for the Florida Association of Realtors reached out directly to me about Karen possibly speaking at the upcoming conference. Though she'd never spoken at a conference, the organizer offered her a $2,500 speaking fee and told her that she could sell anything she wanted to at the conference and keep 100 percent. Best of all, she would be speaking in front of 3,000 real estate professionals. Now, if you know anything about the mortgage business, which is her industry, then you know that mortgage brokers primarily get their clients directly from Realtor referrals. So, there she was being offered to be paid to speak as an authority in front of over 3,000 of her ideal referral partners.

This really lit a fire under Karen, and she decided to get as much publicity as she could. During the next year, Karen was featured on over 100 different radio interviews and podcasts. In fact, there were so many that one of the radio show managers suggested that she should have her own radio show, because she had been so well received. That manager helped Karen create her own show that has since exploded. I spoke to Karen just a few months ago and she told me she now has over 600,000 listeners.

Within a year of all this happening, Karen received an email from an organization that she was a part of, the National Association of Professional Women (NAPW). It reached out to Karen to let her know that because of all that she had done (her bestselling book, her 100-plus radio interviews, her own radio show, and speaking engagements) that she was being awarded the NAPW woman of the year. There was national media attention, due to the fact the organization has over 700,000 members.

Now that's exploding your platform and personal brand.

So, is this really possible to replicate, or is this just a feel-good story and example of what one person can achieve? Well it's certainly a feel-good story, but I can tell you that it's more than possible for you too.

At BSP, we have a full-time PR department to book our clients on media every single week. In fact, we have booked over 1,000 media appearances for our clients in the past four years. Everything from the Howard Stern show to *U.S. News and World Report, Entrepreneur Magazine, Success Magazine, Forbes,* and TV stations (ABC, NBC, CBS, and FOX) from LA to NYC.

So, is it possible to book media? No, it's more than possible. It's definite, if you follow the process and take action

C+(AH+WTS)+H/O = Media

What appears to be a physics equation above is really just our media formula. Let's go through each element together.

C = Credibility

Imagine for a moment you are a producer of a local human-interest story show in San Diego, California (my first TV segment). It's a great place and a top-20 market in the US. As a producer, what is it that you really want? Well, as a producer, you are more than likely wanting to move up the ladder. You want to do bigger shows in bigger markets and make bigger money. You want to move to the number-five market in the US, then the number-two market, and maybe even the number-one market.

Even if you are fully happy in your current market and are not looking to move up, at the least, you certainly don't want to be embarrassed in front of your colleagues by putting someone on the air who is a total disaster or worse, a fraud of some kind. This could ruin your career and make you a laughingstock. So, what do you look for in a guest for your show?

You look for credibility. Your bestselling book checks that box abundantly. You are trustworthy, but that's not enough.

AH+WTS = Audience Hook and Well-Thought-Out Segment

I always recommend to my clients to write a book as focused as possible on your ideal client and niche. This means niching down from the general to the specific.

The problem is that does not work for mass media. (It does for podcasts and blogs though, so this element is specific to mass media.) You see, on mass media they want you to appeal to as broad an audience as possible, otherwise they are not interested.

Recently we featured a client of ours, Ulrik Nerløe on KTLA and KABC in Los Angeles, the number-two market in the US. Ulrik is a productivity consultant to large corporations in Europe and now the US. When preparing Ulrik's pitch to the LA TV stations we could not focus on just his ideal client; we needed to go much broader. So, we created a segment about loving your job and creating a corporate environment that produces that. We tied love to Valentine's Day and the producers loved it. You must create a segment that appeals to the masses for mass media.

A producer is not interested in creating your talking points and your segment for you. You must create catchy points that hook the audience (and first the producer), so the producer knows you are a pro. If he or she gets a pitch that is not well-thought-out or lacking in detail, then they will simply pass and move on to the next pitch.

H and/or O = Hustle and/or Others

Karen didn't get booked on 100-plus media appearances without a lot of work from her team and herself.

You will need to find these opportunities (more on that later), create a catch pitch and segment, contact the producers, and keep working it when some of them say no.

At BSP, we will pitch 10 producers to get one or two bookings, and we're pros at it. Remember PR is free, but there is still a cost involved. You need to hustle to make it happen.

Sources for PR

There are many opportunities for you to do PR, not the least of which is for you to focus on local radio or TV in your own hometown. Here are some resources that can help you find ongoing PR opportunities for yourself and your business.

Cision

If you are serious about PR and perhaps even have an in-house team, then you should look into Cision. Cision is a paid resource database and gives you access to anyone and everyone's information in media. We spend $5,000 per year on this resource and it is invaluable.

Cision is the only paid resource I will suggest. Everything else offers a free version, which works just fine. See https://www.cision.com/us/

HARO

At HARO (Help a Reporter Out), you are able to sign up as a journalist or as a source.

All you need to do is sign up for the basic or free version, which has always worked really well for our clients and us. Remember Bill Stack's virtuous cycle story? Well, all of Bill's media came from the free version of HARO. That's certainly the way that you should get started too.

Set up your HARO account and let service know what you are looking for. HARO will email you queries every day. You get a morning edition and an afternoon edition, and there will be dozens of opportunities.

You simply reply via email with the information that the reporter is asking about you and wait to hear back, that's it! The faster you reply, the better though. Remember there are thousands of others also receiving these queries. See https://www.helpareporter.com/

PitchRate

PitchRate is another simple service.

You can sign up as a journalist or as an expert. You can also connect your profile with your social media. Most of these sites, like HARO and PitchRate, have a fairly big social media presence. See http://pitchrate.com/

I would suggest you also follow these sites on Twitter, Facebook, and LinkedIn. Often, they will tweet (or message) a media request, rather than sending it out via email.

If you follow sites on Twitter or on other social media, then you'll be getting these additional opportunities and resources.

SourceBottle

SourceBottle is similar to HARO and PitchRate. You will sign up as a journalist or as an expert and can upgrade to create an expert profile.

SourceBottle primarily connects journalists and bloggers to experts. It's simple to use and gives you one more, free place to find media opportunities. See https://www.sourcebottle.com/

Podcasts—Blog Talk Radio and Web Talk Radio

At this point in my business, I've personally done every kind of PR, including TV, radio (my own show), print, digital magazines, blogs, and podcasts. These days all I focus on are podcasts, and as I said earlier in this book, I am going all in on that platform and creating my own daily show to continue to grow my platform.

I love podcasts, because of the specificity of the audience. No media comes close to it for return on investment (ROI). I have been on single podcast episodes that have generated over $100,000 in revenue to my company. No other media approaches it for me.

If you are aware of certain podcasts in your niche that would be great for you, then you should certainly follow them on social media and reach out to them for a possible interview. You can also go iTunes and see which podcasts are most popular in your genre. The two sources I am going to mention are simply platforms that can easily be searched for opportunities for you.

Both Blog Talk Radio and WebTalkRadio are great sources for niche-specific opportunities to be on popular podcasts. When you get on their sites, you'll see that you can search all kinds of different categories.

There are tens of thousands of podcasts on Blog Talk Radio, and you are able to search a sub-niche category or you can type your keywords into the search box.

Some examples of niches included are the following.

- Education and family
- Food, fun, pets, and travel
- Health and wellness
- Leadership in the workplace
- Living green
- Love and relationships
- Money and success
- Opinions in culture, politics, and religion
- Sales and marketing

Those are just a few . . . I think you get the point.

There are thousands of shows on these two channels, and they are all looking for experts.

In 2008, when I launched my bestselling book and was looking to grow my brand-new business with it, I still hadn't made a single dime. Well, that's not entirely true. I probably made a few dimes in royalties, but my big break came because I used my book to get on local radio. I used my book to get free publicity.

I've already told the story. It's in an earlier chapter in the book, but just as a reference, understand that your big break could simply be from the free media that you are able to get with your bestselling book. For me, it was radio, but, I tell you, if I were to do that today, my focus would be podcasts and blogs rather than radio and television.

All the growth for my business originated from that first radio show interview that I did and then later grew to my own radio show, paid radio advertising that eventually grew a multimillion-dollar business. You can do this; starting is the hard part.

CHAPTER 12

The Lifeblood of Business

"Selling is something we do for our clients—not to our clients."

—Zig Ziglar

In some ways, everything I've written about up until now leads to this—the lifeblood of our businesses.

Every ad I run, every podcast I am on, every speaking engagement I do, and every book I write (yes, this one too) is about offering value and building awareness that generates leads for my business.

Allow me a moment of sermonizing if you will.

I like to remind my clients that everyone is really in two businesses, not one. The first business is obvious. It's the business of working your magic, doing what you do, and serving the people you love to serve. The second business is less obvious, but in many ways is just as important as your magic. In fact, it is the foundation of the first business.

The second business that you are in is the business of marketing and selling your expertise, your magic. Without the ability to generate leads and create sales, your magic is completely worthless.

If your business is not profitable, if your business is not providing the kind of lifestyle and monetary reward that you deserve, then sooner or later, whatever that business is will become a hobby and you will have to go and get a real job.

You could have the cure for cancer. Yet if you aren't able to monetize it in a way that allows you to focus on it full-time, then what good would it do for anybody?

As I teach, there are only four reasons people do not buy from you. And of the four, one is preeminent.

1. Your prospects don't know if they can trust you.
2. Your prospects don't know if your magic works.
3. Your prospects don't believe in themselves.

And most important—

4. Your prospects don't know you exist.

Your responsibility is to make sure that they know. It's my fault if you don't know me, and I'm bound and determined to make sure that doesn't happen.

Now, the beauty of a book is that it also handles the other three reasons better than anything I have ever come across but that is only secondary to the real issue.

And . . . this is not only about you.

I want you to imagine for a moment that you're sitting in the middle of a group of people. On your left side is a group of people who you are completely responsible to and for. These people are your family members, your spouse, your children, perhaps your mother or father. These are people who count on you to be responsible, to be a servant, to be financially secure.

Those people are also your employees, if you own a business. I think about the people at BSP. They have families to support and their own dreams and goals. Those are the people who have been part of my business for many years and have made a career at BSP. I don't want to let those people down, and to not let them down means that I need to generate leads to continue to grow my business.

If you're not what you need to be, if your business isn't growing, isn't generating leads like it should, then those people suffer. Those people are let down. There's no two ways about it. You're responsible to and for those people.

Now imagine a different group on your right side. Those are your clients who are counting on you. Those are the people who you serve with your magic. Whatever that is, those are the people who are counting on you to make a difference in their lives with your expertise.

Those are the people who paid you. Those are the people who will pay you, because they need the change that you can offer them with your expertise. If you don't reach those people, you do them a disservice. If they don't know that you exist, you do them a disservice.

If you don't approach your business and your expertise in such a way, then it's time to make a change. It's time to stop playing small and instead play big and make a difference in the lives of people like you *can* do.

Read the Zig Ziglar quote again, out loud, to yourself. *"Selling is something we do for our clients—not to our clients."* Do you believe that? Do you have something, some magic that when worked on (or with) others creates amazing results for them? Then it's up to you to let people know.

> It's time to stop playing small and instead play big and make a difference in the lives of people like you *can* do.

Sermon over.

Russell Brunson and Frank Kern are two of the biggest names in the digital marketing space. Russell is a friend, a client of BSP, and I've been a member of his Inner Circle mastermind group for over three years. Frank, I do not personally know, but am also a member of his inner circle newsletter. Both Frank and Russell, independent of each other, have said that their book funnel is the number-one source in their business to generate leads and sales.

Their businesses are actually quite different. Russell's primary business is software as a service (SaaS) called ClickFunnels (of which I am a huge supporter and user), and Russell uses his two bestselling books, *Expert Secrets: The Underground Playbook for Finding Your Message, Building a Tribe, and Changing Your World and DotCom Secrets: The Underground Playbook for Growing Your Company Online* to generate leads. He offers his bestselling books for free, plus a small shipping charge of either $6.95 or $7.95.

After that, buyers are offered a series of upsells and downsells that would be helpful to them. The first upsell is usually an audio version of the book for somewhere between $27 and $37. The second upsell is usually in the range of $97 to $197 and is a digital product that meets a direct need for the potential buyers and eventually they are offered ClickFunnels as either a free trial or discounted for $997 for a set period, including additional training. This business does over $100 million per year in revenue. Yes, you read that correctly.

RUSSELL'S FUNNEL

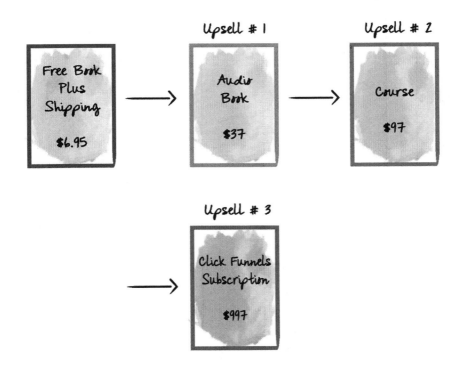

Frank's business is different, but his funnel is actually quite similar. His funnel also starts with his free books. Frank's books are not for sale publicly via Amazon (my personal opinion is that this hurts him overall). All his books are written, published by him, and only for sale on his website or with paid advertising.

His initial offer was for a free softcover copy of the book for a small shipping charge. Recently, Frank has even been offering the book for a small fee and just giving the digital version of the book (not shipping the softcover), and he has said his results are quite promising.

After that, he has a series of upsells that ultimately lead to joining his Inner Circle mastermind program, which costs $397 per month.

Currently, Frank has about 1,200 members in his Inner Circle and produces about $6,000,000 a year in revenue. All this is generated from paid advertising that drives people to his free book offers. Interested yet?

FRANK'S FUNNEL

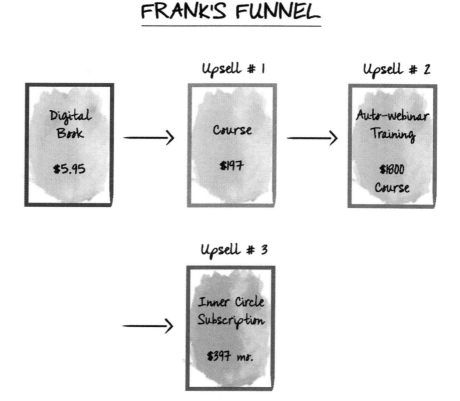

Is this something new? In a word, no.

I remember as a teenager reading a magazine and learning about a company that would give me 12 CDs (actually maybe it was cassettes or even eight tracks, ouch, I am dating myself, aren't I?) for only one penny. I was amazed.

I called the phone number and signed up for Columbia House's amazing offer. The person explained that to be eligible, I'd have to commit to buy a number (12, if I recall) of albums at full price over the next three years. It still seemed like a bargain to me and I went forward. The business acquired a new customer because of an irresistible (almost free) offer.

Columbia House was a $100,000,000 per year business back in the late 1970s and early 1980s. The strategy still works and will continue to work. Human psychology dictates it.

Over the next few pages, I want to share with you some creative ways we have helped our clients to generate leads and grow their businesses using their bestselling books.

Note: Some of the examples I am sharing are time sensitive. Our clients change their funnels regularly, adding and subtracting products to optimize their sales and profit. Something you will want to do also.

Money from a Book *before* the Book Is Written? (Part One)

Taki Moore is an exceptional person, friend, and business coach. He and his wife Kiri-Maree run a successful worldwide coaching business. Taki is known as the coach of coaches.

When it came time for Taki to write his book, we knew it would be a unique process. Many of our clients prefer to craft their books one chapter at a time over a period of a couple of months. Taki, on the other hand, wanted to get it done in just three sessions and to a live audience of his ideal clients. Taki's goal was to actually make money while creating the content for the book. Taki crafted three webinars with the nine key components of his program included. He told his email subscribers and social media followers that he would be doing three webinars to craft the content of his book.

Hundreds registered to be on the webinars, and Taki expertly delivered the content. Telling stories, captivating the audience, and offering his best stuff. Oh, and by the way, he made an offer at the end of each webinar and did over $60,000 in sales *while* creating the content for his book.

A few months later, during the launch of his book, *Million Dollar Coach: The Nine Strategies That Drive a Seven-Figure Coaching Business,* Taki did an additional $350,000 in sales of event tickets, information products, and his signature program, Black Belt.

Today Taki offers the book for free, plus a small shipping charge, to potential clients and gets rave reviews.

TAKI'S FUNNEL

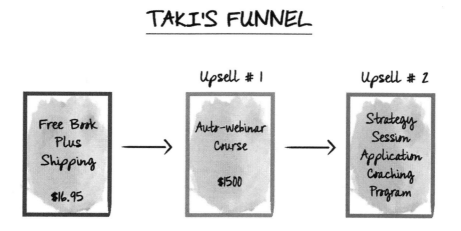

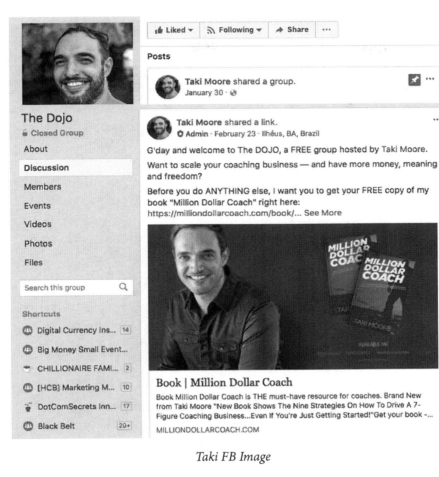

Taki FB Image

Money from a Book *before* the Book Is Written? (Part Two)

My friend and client Matt Theriault is a successful real estate investor and coach to those who wish to learn the ropes of real estate investing.

During the process of helping Matt create his premier bestselling book, we had an idea. What if Matt could help his clients to create additional authority and credibility with a book without them having to write the whole book by themselves?

You see, Matt's clients needed a way to generate leads for their real estate investing businesses and, at the same time, show the homeowners that they were reputable people to deal with. What better way to create leads and authority at the same time than with a book?

So, Matt crafted an offer to his email list and podcast subscribers for them to write a chapter in a new book that Matt would be creating with BSP. They would only need to write one chapter (of the twenty chapters in the book), and we would make the books available to them to print at cost, about $3.50 per book, to use as a lead generator and authority builder.

In just two weeks, Matt sold 20 chapters for $5,000 each, totaling $100,000, and then paid BSP to handle the entire project. Everyone wins, and his clients now have a book that they contributed to that they use to grow their own businesses.

MATT'S MODEL

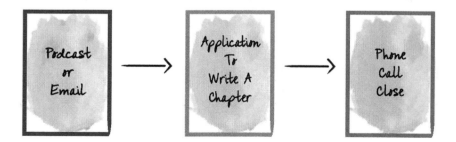

Money from a Book *before* the Book Is Written? (Part Three)

Our client Mia Moran is an exceptional person and action taker. When Mia first came to me to help her craft, publish, and market her cookbook, *Plan Simple Meals" Get More Energy, Raise Healthy Kids, and Enjoy Family Dinner*, she explained that she was planning to raise all the money (and a lot more than needed) by making an offer on the Kickstarter funding platform. Now, to be honest, I had heard this many, many times before and, unfortunately, found that few people ever followed through. The reason I characterized her as an exceptional person and action taker is that she actually did what she said she would.

Though her audience was only moderately sized, her action was not. She launched her book, and during a 30-day period raised over $52,000 on Kickstarter. Far more than she needed to have all the work done for her. We launched her book to bestseller, she grew her audience, and made some fairly good cash while doing it.

Mia now uses her bestselling cookbook to proactively grow her coaching business.

KICKSTARTER

PlanSimple Meals | Family Eating Made Healthy & Gluten-free

PlanSimple Meals — cookbook, meal planner, and parenting handbook — designed to help busy moms make good food for their families.

Created by
Mia Moran

331 backers pledged $52,246 to help bring this project to life.

Book to Booked Call

My dear friend (as I write this, I realize how often I am saying that. So many of my clients have now become dear friends to me. That's cool, well, for me anyway) Shanda Sumpter is a high-level business and marketing coach. I mentioned her in an earlier chapter about her coaching business. Shanda runs a multimillion-dollar business, is the mom of a toddler, and still takes off one week every month.

Shanda generates leads for her business through digital marketing, growing her audience and email list, and her live event (which had over 750 in attendance in 2017, of which I was a featured speaker and sponsor of. Thanks, Shanda).

After we helped her create and launch her bestselling book, *Core Calling*, Shanda began using it to generate leads and sales.

Shanda has a unique approach, offering the book for free as a digital version or for free plus a small shipping fee for the softcover version.

For those who request the free digital download, Shanda requires them to enter their name, email address, and telephone number to receive it. It's your book, so it's your rules.

Shanda then has a follow-up sequence that goes out automatically via email and offers additional content and help in a variety of different ways. Afterwards, her sales team makes outbound calls to every single person who requests a book and offers the person a free coaching call. These calls are consultative sales calls and give the potential client clarity and value. At the end of the call, the individual is offered a chance to join Shanda's $10,000 per year PACE Club coaching program.

The softcover version is offered to people for free, plus the cost of shipping. After they enter their credit card to pay for shipping, they are offered a list-growing program that Shanda sells for $197. Whether they take that offer or not, they are then offered another program for $997, her proprietary sales course, ISOLVE. After they complete their purchase, they are called and offered a free coaching call and afterwards, if they are a fit, are offered Shanda's $10,000 coaching program.

In the first four months of using her book and this process, she generated over 11,572 leads (of which 7,763 gave their telephone numbers) and sold over $409,000 in coaching services.

It's worth mentioning that Shanda's programs are highly effective and over 60 percent of her PACE Club graduates move on to her $20,000 program, Marketing Mastery, to continue growing their businesses with Shanda's help.

SHANDA'S FUNNEL

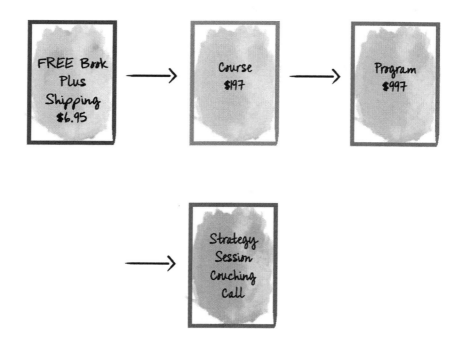

Book to High-Ticket Franchise Sales

Jim Hansen is one of the foremost experts in the country on franchise growth. As the former CEO of franchising for Subway International, Jim oversaw a $600,000,000 per year budget and Subway's growth from six stores to over 20,000 franchise locations.

When Jim decided to leave Subway for a new franchise opportunity, it would be easy to assume that his new franchise would explode too. Initially though, Jim found that his ideal clients were far less trusting of a new opportunity than they were for an established name brand like Subway.

Which is not hard to understand, when you consider who the ideal franchise buyer is. In many cases, the franchise buyer is someone who has been working for a number of years, perhaps in a corporation in a leadership capacity, is desirous of branching out on his or her own, and has a nest egg of funds to invest. Most of the franchise's marketing was focused on airline magazines, because many corporation executives are traveling from place to place for their company.

Our idea was to help Jim create a book about his expertise, franchising, and so we helped him launch his bestseller, *Secrets of Choosing the Right Franchise: Your Guide to Researching, Selecting and Buying the Franchise of Your Dreams*, to be used to build trust and generate leads for his new opportunity.

The behind-the-scenes thinking was that the franchise buyer was extra cautious because this was his or her only shot to get it right, using retirement savings and a nest egg to start the business. The buyer had every reason to trust Jim because of his years of experience growing Subway, but if he was simply contacting the buyer in the capacity of sales for his franchise, then his or her guard would automatically go up.

Jim's bestselling book now positions him as America's franchise coach, adding an entire layer of credibility and authority before he ever spoke to a potential franchisee. Sales immediately exploded. Here is what Jim had to say.

> *I only get better by being with players who are better than me, an atmosphere where people are striving for excellence. That's what Rob's group does. In the last 90 days, I've produced $178,600 in income and a lot of it has to do with the work I'm doing with Rob.*

If you are selling anything of high value and high investment, then getting your bestselling book in the hands of your prospects will massively increase your credibility and authority and do the heavy lifting for you. Especially if you have your book filled with helpful information and great client case studies.

Book to Information Product

Kaelin Tuell Poulin and her husband Brandon are business and marketing masters. Kaelin turned her personal life transformation into a multimillion-dollar business serving more than 1.3 million clients worldwide.

Kaelin transformed her life with diet and exercise, losing 65 pounds. She became the fastest woman ever to go from amateur to professional International Federation of BodyBuilders (IFBB). I was honored to help her get her story out in her bestselling book, *Big Fat Lies*, which became the number-one book on all of Barnes and Noble, outselling the number one nonfiction author in the country (Bill O'Reilly), and also Tony Robbins and a host of other successful authors.

Our PR department then booked Kaelin on a national TV tour to highlight the book and her program's success. She tracked her daily journey on her social media following (750,000 people) and actually started having fans show up at the TV stations ahead of her interviews to celebrate with her.

Kaelin now offers her bestselling book for free, plus a small shipping charge. (Are you seeing a pattern here?) After the book buyers submit their information, they are offered the first upsell option, an audio version of the book (usually $27 to $37). The second upsell is for a higher price program for $147. This simple funnel produced over $100,000 in sales in the first month alone and has continued to produce amazing results.

Kaelin and Brandon now offer a higher-priced coaching program and a monthly supplement subscription.

KAELIN'S FUNNEL

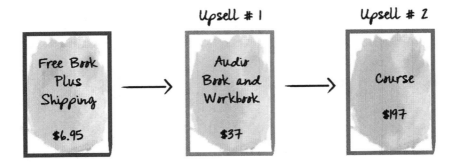

Profitable Client Acquisition

Jeff Barnes came to us to help him launch and market his financial advice book, *The Ultimate Guide to Self-Directed Investing and Retirement Planning: Control Your Financial Future, Self-Direct Your Investments, Create a Tax-Free "Bulletproof" Wealth Plan, and Live the Life You Want!* Jeff's goal was to use his book to generate leads for his investing partnership and online sales of his information products and consulting services.

We launched Jeff's book to international bestseller and then helped him secure media opportunities on radio, podcasts, and print. As I tell all my clients, once your book is a bestseller, it's time to focus the media and platform opportunities on you and whatever it is you are offering and selling. With the focus on using the book to find potential clients, Jeff created a lead generation program for his offer with his book as the primary lead magnet.

Jeff's goal was to find high net worth individuals who were interested in his expertise of self-directed invested. In the first month, Jeff attracted over 1,000 leads using his book as the front-end offer. Jeff then followed up with them via email and offered an eight-week program to learn the ins and out of self-directed investing for $2,500. He sold 20 spots totaling $50,000 in revenue and began his program.

After the eight-week course, Jeff and his partner then offered qualified clients the opportunity to invest with them in various real estate projects they had vetted. They raised over $5,000,000 from these individuals for the various projects they had and went from book to program to profit partners.

JEFF'S FUNNEL

Upsell # 1   Upsell # 2

```
┌──────────┐         ┌──────────┐         ┌──────────┐
│          │         │Consultative│        │          │
│  Free    │   ──>   │ Coaching │   ──>    │Partnership│
│ Digital  │         │Call/Sale │         │ Offer To │
│  Book    │         │          │         │Qualified │
│          │         │  $2500   │         │Individuals│
└──────────┘         └──────────┘         └──────────┘
```

Growing the Brand and Balance Sheet Together

Kevin Harrington has become a household name in most business and marketing circles. As I related earlier in the book, he was the original shark on the hit TV show *Shark Tank*, the inventor of the infomercial, and the man who brought us everything from Ginsu knives to the George Foreman grill.

Kevin originally told me the story sitting on a boat in Newport Beach harbor back in 2016. He had earned millions of dollars selling products on TV infomercials, but things began to change, starting in the mid-2000s in the television market. Television market share began plummeting, while advertising prices remained the same and even increased. With an ever-lessening viewership on TV, product sales on infomercials also began dropping, and a once-profitable business model started to fade away.

At that time, he had a powerful discussion with someone he describes as a friend and mentor of his, Sir Richard Branson, founder of the

Virgin Group. Richard told him for the longest time he didn't even know who Kevin was because he was always behind the scenes, but with the landscape changing to digital marketing he should take the opportunity to change his business model and start building his own brand.

In 2009, Kevin published his first book, *Act Now! How I Turn Ideas into Million-Dollar Products*. Kevin has now gone all in on positioning and personal branding. He speaks 50–75 times per year all over the world and has partnered and digitally launched some amazing products and programs (most recently partnering with the late Zig Ziglar's estate).

My company runs the digital advertising campaigns, using Kevin's previous books and videos that he and I have done to generate leads and opportunities. We run the ads on Facebook, offering information about the opportunity. After watching a brief video, people are invited to fill out an application to speak with one of our author development coaches. If the person is qualified, our author development coach then explains the opportunity and investment, and they either move forward or not. In the first eight months of this partnership, we have generated thousands of leads and done over $250,000 in revenue.

KEVIN'S FUNNEL

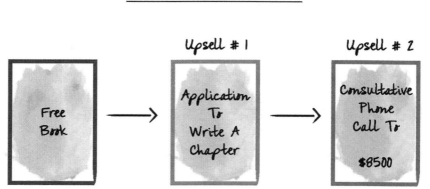

Conclusion

These are just a few of the ways our clients are using their books to grow their brand and income with their bestselling books. The key to every story is the proactive focus of the authors to create the results that you see. These things did not happen by accident nor can *any* real or prolonged result happen accidentally.

Many of our clients will experience a (temporary) boost in lead generation, speaking opportunities, and publicity when their book launches. This is great and is the proverbial icing on the cake, but this is written for you to have dozens of different examples that you can follow and put your own unique twist on.

> The key to every story is the proactive focus of the authors to create the results that you see.

Find ways to get your book into your ideal client's hands. Every potential client should have a copy of your book mailed to them. Put a sticky note on it and personalize it. Let them know after your phone call with them that you realized you had a similar example to theirs on page 122 (or whatever) and direct them to it. You will be selling without ever having to sell.

Get your book into your past client's hands to re-engage them with you. Get your book to your current clients to pass on to friends and family or anyone that they might refer. Find ways to use your book. Only your imagination is the limit.

CHAPTER 13

Tick Tock, Tick Tock

"All I need is a sheet of paper and something to write with, and then I can turn the world upside down."

—Friedrich Nietzsche

Several years ago, a friend called me with a dilemma. He runs a great business and serves an upscale clientele with needed products and services. His big issue at the time was that his business was primarily built on his sphere of influence and referrals from friends and past clients. Hard to scale a business like that and sometimes hard to know where (and when) the next client is coming from.

The dilemma? Well, he had a great referral from a past client who was thrilled with his results and so referred a friend who was in need of the exact same service. All good, so far. By the way, I am purposely leaving out the details of his business for privacy and, honestly, it doesn't matter to the point of the story at all. This could be any business, anywhere. In fact, it might sound a lot like yours.

As you might imagine, his closing rate on a referral like this was darn near 100 percent. After all, what's better than a great referral? The problem? He lost the potential client to a less-qualified (his words) competitor. Of course, I asked him if he followed up with the referral and asked what happened. He said that he called and asked the person why he decided to go with his competitor after he received such a glowing recommendation to use his services. The referral's answer? Four words, "He had a book."

I'd love to tell you a great ending, that now my friend also has a book, and everything is amazing in his business. Truth be told, he doesn't. Oh, he was certainly motivated to write one when he lost that referral, but you know, motivation wanes.

So, what happened? Who knows? Life, business, a new shiny object? What I know and see on a weekly basis is that writing a book is hard. Really hard.

Remember in Chapter 1, when I told you that the *New York Times* did a survey and found that 81 percent of adult Americans wanted to write a book? It's hard to say if 81 percent of all Americans should really write a book, but that is another question for another day. The fact is they want to. That you also want to actually puts you in the majority, not the minority.

A better fact, perhaps, is that only about 1 percent of people ever accomplish this goal—from 81 percent to 1 percent. That puts you in rarified air, if and when you actually get it done.

The problem, as I've outlined in the earlier chapters, is the model itself. The model to write, publish, promote, and profit from a book has been broken for a long time and only more recently have better opportunities appeared. The old Author 1.0 model is broken, but now you have a better way to get your book published and make it extraordinarily successful.

Again, the three primary elements to getting everything you want accomplished with a book, we call Publish. Promote. Profit. If you are stuck somewhere in the process, then more than likely it is because you are still using Author 1.0 in that area.

Being stuck in Publish 1.0 means you are grinding daily over thousands of words, often without a clear direction, and then hoping for a traditional publishing deal.

The solution in Publish 2.0 is to build a great foundation for your content, use a hybrid ghostwriting system to create content and then utilize Amazon as your publishing platform. (Refer to Section One.)

If you are worried about promoting your book, then you are stuck in a Promote 1.0 mentality, afraid you need to have a large platform in place to market your book. If you have one, that's great, more power to you, if not, then no problem.

> The three primary elements to getting everything you want accomplished with a book, we call Publish. Promote. Profit.

Promote 2.0 turns the traditional model on its head. Instead of needing a platform to launch your book, we are actually going to use your book to build tour following and platform. Oh, and you'll become a bestseller in the process. (Refer to Section Two.)

Are you overly worried about royalties? Sorry to say that you are stuck in Profit 1.0. You are more than likely not going to sell hundreds of thousands or millions of books. If you do, awesome, if not, no problem. I've shown you dozens of examples of people earning hundreds of thousands and millions of dollars without royalties.

In Profit 2.0, we ignore the royalties (they still come in on their own though) and instead focus on using our books to attract speaking engagements, PR, and to generate leads for our businesses. (Refer to Section Three.)

As I've outlined on the pages of this book, we live in a new world now. A world of Author 2.0. Exciting times these are!

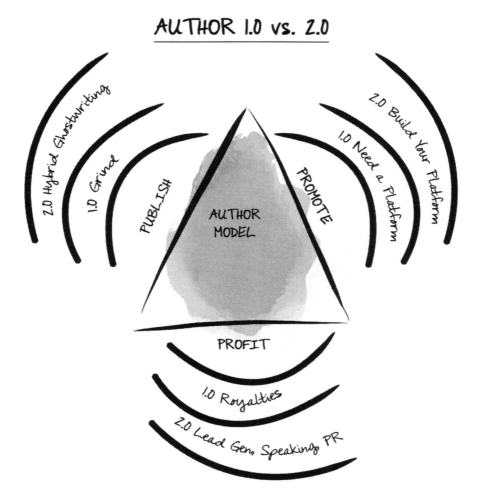

AUTHOR 1.0 vs. 2.0

As a final word, I'm often asked by my clients when the right time is to launch their books. Should they wait until the new year? Perhaps launch during summer? Christmas maybe?

My answer is always simple and to the point. The *best* time to write and launch your book was 10 years ago. The second-best time is right now. With the steps outlined in this book, there is no reason you cannot have your book written and launched in the next 60–90 days.

Your competitors might be in the process of writing their books right now, slaving away in Author 1.0. You have the knowledge. What will you do with it? Tick tock, tick tock.

> With the steps outlined in this book, there is no reason you cannot have your book written and launched in the next 60–90 days.

About the Author

Rob Kosberg is a 3 time best selling author, and the founder of www. BestSellerPublishing.org. He has been featured on ABC, NBC, CBS, Fox, Forbes and Entrepreneur magazine as well as hundreds of other shows, podcasts, magazines and articles.

Rob's Publish.Promote.Profit.™ system has been used by thousands of authors in dozens of countries. He shows entrepreneurs how to become the go-to authority in their market by writing, launching and profiting with a best selling book.

Since 2010, Rob has been the go-to teacher for coaches, consultants and entrepreneurs who want more authority, more exposure, and more clients. Rob works with clients who understand that the way to 7 figures and beyond is via a best selling book and authority and celebrity that comes with it.

Connect with Me

https://www.facebook.com/robkosberg

https://www.facebook.com/robkosbergcoaching/

https://twitter.com/robkosberg

http://bestsellerpublishing.org/